theatre & education

Helen Nicholson

palgrave
macmillan

First published 2009 by
PALGRAVE MACMILLAN

Palgrave Macmillan in the UK is an imprint of Macmillan
Publishers Limited, registered in England, company number
785998, of Houndmills, Basingstoke, Hampshire RG21 6XS.

Palgrave Macmillan in the US is a division of St Martin's Press LLC,
175 Fifth Avenue, New York, NY 10010.

Palgrave Macmillan is the global academic imprint of the above
companies and has companies and representatives throughout
the world.

Palgrave® and Macmillan® are registered trademarks in the United
States, the United Kingdom, Europe and other countries.

ISBN-13: 978-0-230-21857-4 paperback
ISBN-10: 0-230-21857-1 paperback

This book is printed on paper suitable for recycling and made
from fully managed and sustained forest sources. Logging,
pulping and manufacturing processes are expected to conform to
the environmental regulations of the country of origin.

A catalogue record for this book is available from the British
Library.

A catalog record for this book is available from the Library of
Congress.

10 9 8 7 6 5 4 3 2
18 17 16 15 14 13 12 11 10

Printed and bound in China

contents

series editors' preface

The theatre is everywhere, from entertainment districts to the fringes, from the rituals of government to the ceremony of the courtroom, from the spectacle of the sporting arena to the theatres of war. Across these many forms stretches a theatrical continuum through which cultures both assert and question themselves.

Theatre has been around for thousands of years, and the ways we study it have changed decisively. It's no longer enough to limit our attention to the canon of Western dramatic literature. Theatre has taken its place within a broad spectrum of performance, connecting it with the wider forces of ritual and revolt that thread through so many spheres of human culture. In turn, this has helped make connections across disciplines; over the past fifty years, theatre and performance have been deployed as key metaphors and practices with which to rethink gender, economics, war, language, the fine arts, culture and one's sense of self.

Theatre & is a long series of short books which hopes to capture the restless interdisciplinary energy of theatre and performance. Each book explores connections between theatre and some aspect of the wider world, asking how the theatre might illuminate the world and how the world might illuminate the theatre. Each book is written by a leading theatre scholar and represents the cutting edge of critical thinking in the discipline.

We have been mindful, however, that the philosophical and theoretical complexity of much contemporary academic writing can act as a barrier to a wider readership. A key aim for these books is that they should all be readable in one sitting by anyone with a curiosity about the subject. The books are challenging, pugnacious, visionary sometimes and, above all, clear. We hope you enjoy them.

Jen Harvie and Dan Rebellato

foreword

This is a wide-ranging but precise account of the movement for creating theatre for young audiences. It records its history and examines its various, often conflicting, philosophies. Latterly it developed with a rapidity that was sometimes bewildering. But this is a complement to its vitality. Its practitioners saw it as their responsibility to relate to the major events that affected young people's lives. It was the time of the post-Second World War, the first Labour government's educational reforms, the cold war, the collapse of communism, the explosion of 'consumerism', the interlude of the 'peace dividend', and the present dangers of ecological and economic disaster, extremism and terrorism. The frontline now runs by the gateway of every school.

This new situation is different. In the past, all the movement's various practices were related to theories that had their origins in other parts of society: political, psychological, social, pedagogic theories in general. Each theory could be claimed as a coherent basis for young people's theatre. This is no longer so. We are at a crossroads without signposts. This is not just the curse of post-modernism, it is a fact that the human species no longer knows how to manage its affairs.

So we have to ask fundamental questions about drama *sui generis*. Why did our species create the arts of theatre? Why the awesome categories of Tragedy and Comedy? What made theatre so fundamental to civilization?

Helen Nicholson describes *Boychild*, a skilfully created event in Portland, a port in the UK. Its 'exhibits' included a teenager in pyjamas lying on a beautifully-lit heap of unwashed potatoes as a recording of a poem was played—parts of human bodies in bread made by participants under the supervision of a master baker—the sorts of things that might have originated in an American 'happening' (also described) in which a pianist poured water from one bucket into another while old records were played on a hand-wound gramophone. *Boychild* was intended to help young males handle problems of masculinity. One young participant spoke of his extreme excitement, but he could have got that in other ways. Really, there is nothing in the event which would prevent a boy saying, 'well in that case, I'll become a Nazi and beat up Pakis'. The organisers would ensure that this didn't happen, but to do so they would have to go beyond the parameters of their event. It is an illusion to suppose that aesthetic events instigate moral or rational imperatives.

Pouring water from one bucket into another in an American college means one thing, in an African village in a drought it means another thing. Is there something you can do for boys in Portland that would have as vital an import in their lives as pouring water would in an African village?

The text also describes my play *The Children*. I have not seen *Boychild*. It may well do better what it sets out to do than *The Children* does. I am analysing only intentions. The event and the play are based on radically different understandings of what human beings are and why they have created the institutions of drama. We had to create drama in order to be conscious and human. It is not a matter of reflection, Brechtian or otherwise. Put roughly, drama uses the same emotional and intellectual—psycho-physical—means by which, from birth onwards, and critically during childhood, each of us creates a 'self'. Those means are inherent in consciousness, and so the site of drama is the site of consciousness: each moment of drama contains both the kitchen table and the edge of the universe. Because living is exigent, drama imposes on you a choice in which you define yourself in relation to the totality of that site. You can never escape the responsibility of being on it. That is the knowledge of childhood which adults may forget in the contrivances of survival.

This is a very helpful book. It records the movement's history and brings us to its present crossroads. We must distinguish between drama and theatre. Both may be used well so long as they are not confused with each other. *Boychild* is theatre, *The Children* is drama. Theatre can teach, drama teaches nothing—drama *creates* in the strict sense I've described. The aesthetic is given cognitive meaning only in drama, a truth which an age of irresponsibility denied. Theatre may help you to find yourself in society, drama requires you to find society in you. To find, that is, your humanness and accept responsibility for being human. Then the rest will follow. The difference between theatre and drama is absolute. A category which tries to contain both is too broad to be useful. This confusion has all but destroyed adult theatres, which have become show shops for shop shows. If we do not make the distinction for children we will turn childhood into a commodity.

Edward Bond is an internationally renowned playwright whose works include Saved, Lear, The Sea, Bingo, The Woman, *and* The War Plays. *Since the early 1990s he has written several plays for young people, including* At the Inland Sea, Eleven Vests, The Children. *and* Tune.

theatre & education

Theatre and childhood memories

My first experience of theatre was a pantomime of *Cinderella* at Golders Green Hippodrome in London in 1962. I was three. I can still picture the comedian Arthur Askey as Buttons, dressed in a dark-blue footman's costume with a matching pill-box hat, telling jokes to a good-humoured audience. I can even remember the jokes, not so much because I understood them at the time but because they were repeated so often by my father that they became integrated into our family history. To my surprise the programme was recently available on eBay, and my enthusiastic two-quid bid secured me a piece of history that promised to revive memories of that enchanting matinee. When the programme arrived, my attention was drawn to the eclecticism of the adverts rather than information about the performance. Corsetière Mme H. Lieberg presented 'her exclusive collection of international foundation garments', Gilberts Furs Ltd. offered to repair and remodel fur coats, and, as part of London University's Extension programme, there were to be '10 Lantern lectures' about archaeological exploration. The advertisers were clearly expecting a more affluent audience than my family, and we didn't take advantage of these exclusive offers. Theatre was a rare and expensive treat, and, sitting on the edge of my tipped-up seat watching a glittering Cinderella go to the ball, I can remember thinking that I was lucky to witness such a magical spectacle.

My next memory of theatre is when a group of actors came to perform in my primary school. It must have been about 1964. The school was newly built, having moved from a dark Victorian building where the outside lavatories froze in winter to a bright and airy building with a light hall that had a glass dome in the ceiling. I think the play had something to do with fairy-tale characters, though the details of the plot are hazy. I do vividly remember the thrill of being so close to the actors that I could talk to them, touch their brightly coloured costumes and see the laughter creases in their thick clowns' make-up. What seemed remote, inaccessible and impossibly glamorous at Golders Green suddenly seemed within my grasp. Here were real actors in my school, asking us questions and occasionally expecting us to join in the story. My class formed a sizeable audience of forty-eight six-year-olds, and I remember that the teacher, whom we called Mrs Grumpy, took one boy out of the room for ignoring the drama and running round pretending to be a motorbike. I rather regret calling my teacher Mrs Grumpy. I expect teaching forty-eight six-year-olds every day would test anyone's patience.

Nearly twenty years later, as a teacher myself, I took a class of twelve-year-olds on a coach to participate in a Theatre-in-Education programme devised by Bush Telegraph Theatre Company in Bristol, directed by Alistair Moir. As we arrived at the venue, two actors staggered onto the coach asking the children to hide them urgently under their coats. The bemused bus driver was forced to drive around the semi-derelict docks to face the aggressive questioning of an actor in role as an armed soldier. Bristol docks had become Poland's revolutionary Lenin Shipyard in Gdańsk, and it was 1982, the year in which the anti-communist Solidarity trade union movement (Solidarność) was banned by the Soviet government that controlled Poland at the time. The trade unionists we had protected on the bus told us about their experiences and explained how their lives were affected by the current political situation. Informed by this teaching, we were ushered into a disused warehouse where we were invited to help print bold, anti-Soviet posters in sticky red ink. A moment of exquisite drama unfolded as the warehouse was raided by the Polish police, and we were bundled back onto our bus as our new trade-union friends were led away. Returning back to England (or, more precisely, to the arts venue round the corner), we were invited to give our impressions of our Polish 'holiday' to reporters, whose inane questioning about the food, weather and night-life made the young people incandescent with rage. They had a story to tell about social injustice, and the memorable morning ended with the young people recording their own commentaries to TV footage of the events they had witnessed.

Many of us have vivid memories of our early encounters with theatre, perhaps when the visit of a theatre company or a trip to the theatre broke the daily routine of school life. Working with a group of actors in school, taking part in a performance or visiting a theatre often remains indelibly imprinted on young people's memories. I have chosen to begin this book with my own memories of three theatre events in part because they are evocative of performances that took place in the historical period that is discussed in this book. More particularly, however, I have chosen them because they represent different modes of professional theatre that continue to touch the lives of young people. Many children are entertained by the popular and commercial theatre, whether by the spectacle of Christmas pantomimes or by lavish musicals, where the production is marketed to children and family audiences. The second example is significant insofar as the performance took place within a primary school rather than a theatre building, a move that was designed to counteract the perceived inaccessibility and élitism of commercial theatre by inviting every child in the class to enjoy the experience of theatre and take a small role in the story. The third example, a site-specific performance, was explicitly intended to contribute to young people's political and social education. Participating in this drama positioned young people as witnesses to a significant moment in history and drew attention to their role as social actors within a wider political sphere. Even allowing for the haziness of my recollections, these three snapshots of practice provide insights into the different values that motivate practitioners who make theatre that engages young people.

This book is about the contribution professional theatre practitioners make to education. It is possible to learn from *all* theatre, of course, but that does not mean that all theatre is explicitly designed to be educational. Even the commercial theatre, famously dismissed by Bertolt Brecht for its lack of educational and social function, can provide opportunities to learn. An aspiring comedian attending that *Cinderella* matinee, for example, might have learnt from close observation of Arthur Askey's expert comic timing, or a performance studies scholar might choose the production to analyse the performer–audience relationship in popular theatre. In other words, all performances can provide opportunities to those with an interest in learning about theatre. Many theatre-makers who choose to work in educational settings intend, however, to make a difference to all young people, whether or not they are interested in the theatre as a craft or as a cultural practice. It is this more general aspiration towards using theatre as a learning medium and a vehicle of social betterment that has inspired generations of practitioners to contribute to the education of young people.

It is in part because theatre is such a memorable medium that the educational and aesthetic principles that inform its practices have been subject to continual discussion and lively debate. Practitioners have always responded to the contexts and times in which they are working, and in this book I sketch some of paradigm shifts, tensions and

opportunities that have affected the ways in which professional theatre-makers have worked with young people. It
is important to underline the scope and limits of this book
and to clarify where it sits within the field. This book is concerned with professional theatre that is explicitly designed
to contribute to young people's education, and, as such, it
is not primarily about Theatre for Children, a movement
established in the twentieth century by pioneers such as
Winifred Ward, Nellie McCaslin and Lowell Swortzell in
the United States and Caryl Jenner and Brian Way in the
United Kingdom. According to Nellie McCaslin, in her
essay 'History of Children's Theatre in the United States'
(1961), children's theatre had 'the express purpose of giving
children wholesome pleasure' (p. 21). Although some children's theatre now has links to education, its major function
remains family entertainment rather than education. Nor is
the teaching of drama the central focus of this book, even
though drama teachers have undoubtedly influenced the
pedagogy of professional theatre-makers who work in education. Furthermore, this book does not attempt a comprehensive survey of theatre and education in different parts of
the world. It is inevitably bound up in my own experience of
theatre in various formal and informal educational settings
in the United Kingdom – as a pupil in the 1960s and 1970s,
as a drama teacher in schools in the 1980s and early 1990s
and, more recently, as a researcher and practitioner.

Collaborations between practitioners and policy-makers
have led to ideas and practices being shared, interpreted and
revised for different contexts, and this means there is no

one movement or single set of practices that can be used to measure or define contemporary fusions of theatre and education. On the contrary, there are multiple forms of theatre that are intended to stimulate and challenge young people, only some of which can be captured in this book. It is, however, precisely because theatre is applied in many different ways to education that its values, politics and performance methodologies need to be continually questioned, revitalised and renewed. This book is intended to make a contribution to that process.

Debating theatre and education

> Artistic creation is so unstable that a theatre seems to me the last place you would go to 'learn' something.
>
> Howard Barker, *Arguments for a Theatre* (1997), p. 137

> Education should enable children to search for meaning so that they may bear witness to life.
>
> Edward Bond, 'The Dramatic Child' (1997), p. 91

Although it has many advocates, not all contemporary theatre-makers are enthusiastic about collaboration between theatre and education. The quotations with which I began this section, taken from the writings of two influential British playwrights, illustrate very different attitudes to the coupling of theatre and education. Howard Barker rejects the idea that theatre can educate without seriously compromising its artistic values, a view shared by the US playwright David Mamet. Edward Bond, on the other hand, suggests that educational theatre offers a dynamic place to pose essential questions about the human condition. It is worth examining both sides of the argument, not least because some critics of educational theatre have powerful voices within professional theatre across the world.

In his cultural manifesto *Arguments for a Theatre* (1997), Barker makes a powerful case for a theatre that he describes as 'rebellious', free from function and serving no utilitarian purpose. His analysis of contemporary theatre is damning, and his argument is based on the view that theatre is artistically constrained by the obligation either to entertain or to educate. He states that today's theatre is sterile because it has become, respectively, either an 'industry with a market' or a 'social service with a popular obligation' (p. 146). Whether theatre is a commercial enterprise charged with making money or is tied to educational objectives and social agendas, Barker insists that the imperative to satisfy the consequent perceived interests and needs leads to uncreative and unimaginative work. By placing consumers or students at the centre of the creative process rather than the actors, both versions of theatre become, in Barker's view, intellectually and artistically impoverished.

Barker paints a picture of a contemporary theatre that is responsive to a society 'obsessed with profit and enlightenment, with populism and access' (p. 146). Although he recognises that theatre education (enlightenment and access, in Barker's terms) and the commercialisation of theatre (profit and popularism) are motivated by different values, he remains critical of a culture industry that is regulated by the power of conscience or the demands of commerce. In Barker's words, the art of theatre is unpredictable and instinctive; it 'invents life', whereas a theatre that is driven by commerce or education can succeed only in reproducing life as it is already known and understood. He argues for a theatre that breaks this dual stranglehold:

> *Not to know* admits a willing surrender of the crit-
> ical faculty so beloved of educational theatre ... *not*
> *to enjoy* announces a fracturing of the transactional
> values of the entertainment industry. (p. 148)

As an alternative, Barker advocates a theatre that relishes the unstable and irrational aspects of creativity and that seeks to challenge certainty by exploring the more painful or troubling qualities of the poetic imagination.

It is interesting to note that Howard Barker, an experimental playwright, makes the assumption that educational theatre is inevitably tied to aesthetic principles and dramatic structures that militate against the artistic exploration of complexity and ambiguity. Furthermore, he presumes that all education is predictable and didactic, and this means that, according to Barker's logic, educational theatre is inevitably concerned with imparting simple messages rather than asking provocative questions or, indeed, encouraging young people's creativity. Of course, there are some couplings of theatre and education that would stand guilty as charged. In a 2004 article in the *Guardian* newspaper entitled 'Where's the Challenge?', the playwright David Edgar attacked the British government's arts policies, citing Theatre-in-Education as a specific example of how arts funding has been directed towards delivering predetermined targets: 'Small theatre-in-health-education theatre groups,' Edgar claims, have been given 'checklists of morally improving messages to insert into plays about bullying'. Although this may be an unfair caricature of educational theatre, it is uncomfortably recognisable as a trait of some funded work. Theatre can be used to drive home particular information, elucidate specific issues or impart moral certitudes, thereby leaving little scope for the imaginative, aesthetic or creative involvement of young people. But this trivialisation of both education and theatre is only part of the story.

One of the most influential advocates of contemporary educational theatre is another British playwright, Edward Bond. Bond shares Barker's pessimism about the commodification of theatre and similarly holds consumerism responsible for the current loss of the social imagination. Unlike Barker, however, Bond responds to the moral corruption he sees in society by arguing that it is imperative that theatre educates the imagination by asking radical questions, and he advocates a theatrical pedagogy that is specifically oriented towards young people. In his essay 'Notes on Theatre-in-Education' (2000), Bond argues that 'imagination changes reality' and that educational theatre thus has a vital role in encouraging children to imagine a future that is free from social injustice:

> Bad drama flourishes in an unjust society. Our future always depends on the state of our imaginations. Drama becomes more important as the world changes. Theatre is just or corrupt and in the urgency of the times there is nothing in between. That is because theatre is the place where reality is made real. The plays young people write, act and watch are blueprints of the world they will have to live in. (p. 58)

This alliance between theatre, social justice and education is politically charged and optimistic; engagement with theatre has the potential to encourage young people to become, in the terms Bond uses in 'The Dramatic Child' (1997), 'competent members of a critical culture' (p. 86). For Bond, a just society lies in the hands of children who have conjoined rational criticism with imaginative freedom, and his dramatic output has become increasingly focused on that educational imperative.

Debates about the elision between theatre and education drive at the heart of why theatre matters. It is significant that Barker and Bond, albeit from different perspectives and aesthetic traditions, share a concern about the power of the imagination and the need for theatre to bear witness to the serious struggles of life. Live theatre that seeks to challenge conventional modes of thought and feeling is often perceived to be under threat, and although the focus of theatre-makers' questions and the stories they tell varies over time, an independent and politically engaged artistic culture is often regarded as one of the markers of a thriving democracy. Seen in this light, the resistance of theatre-makers and teachers to 'delivering' the government's social and educational agendas through theatre is entirely understandable; theatre-makers frequently regard themselves as independent-minded cultural provocateurs rather than uncritical followers of government agendas. But if the condition of theatre says something about the state of democracy, then the education of a society's young citizens speaks even louder about its values. A market-led culture of individualism has seeped into education policies as well as cultural practice, and target-setting, personalised learning and school league tables have been promoted, often at the expense of collaborative learning methods, risk-taking and non-competitive approaches to educational provision. It is unsurprising that, within an educational climate that promotes individualism and has charged the arts with healing social division, the role of theatre in educational contexts has become subject to close critical scrutiny.

One way to make sense of how the contemporary synthesis of theatre and education has been shaped is to locate its values and working methods within the context of wider theatrical histories and educational cultures. Theatrical experiments in educational settings are complexly interwoven with the dramatic and educational innovations of their day, and thus the practices of theatre educationalists often offer insights into why theatre was considered a necessity in its time and how it spoke to the culture and society of the period. Crucially, because theatre that seeks to engage young people looks to the future, it often articulates a vision of social change and educational aspirations. Contemporary practitioners in the field of theatre and education are indebted, therefore, to a rich history of theatrical experimentation that was fuelled by political discussion and, sometimes, both marred and enriched by dispute and divisions. In the following sections I revisit this history, tracing some of the educational and political principles that inspired previous generations of theatre-makers in order to shed some light on the continuities and discontinuities between past and present practices.

The theatre in educational history

The theatre is implicated in two parallel and inter-related educational movements, drama-in-education and Theatre-in-Education, both of which gained strength after the Second World War and became particularly influential in the era of optimism of the 1960s. Perhaps paradoxically, it was when drama and theatre became more integrated into the curriculum that education developed an increasingly ambiguous relationship with the theatre as a cultural institution. This apparent contradiction is explained in part by the fact that, in the post-war period, education was seen as a major force for social change; a comprehensive state education system and non-hierarchical teaching methods became an important symbol of post-war democracy. The commercialism and conservatism of mainstream theatre, in contrast, were regarded with suspicion by those whose serious-minded ambition was to promote social equality through an inclusive education system.

The introduction of drama into the daily working practices of schools during this period aimed to develop an alternative pedagogy built on principles of play and collaborative learning rather than teaching children about the theatre as a cultural practice. British drama-in-education and Creative Dramatics in the United States owed much to the principles of progressive education, a movement that stressed the centrality of the child in the learning process and advocated classroom environments in which children were encouraged to express themselves spontaneously and freely, without fear of social constraints. Although drama-in-education and Creative Dramatics were differently inflected, both marked a significant shift from the more passive and hierarchical forms of learning that had hitherto dominated education.

Particularly influential on the development of progressive education was the work of the American philosopher John Dewey (1859–1952). Dewey argued that children's cognitive and emotional development was best supported by constructive childhood play and problem-solving, and this attitude to learning prompted a revolution in educational thinking in which the arts had a central role. Participating in the arts, Dewey suggested, is a playful experience that, when introduced into education, enables children to make links between their own imaginative worlds and the learning environment of school. His book *Art as Experience* (1934) offered an aesthetic philosophy that paved the way for subsequent educationalists to understand how the practice of the arts might be integrated into children's learning. One of Dewey's arguments was that the arts have the special ability to integrate children's thoughts and feelings with their actions – a process that, in Dewey's terms, brings together the child's internal subjectivity and the external world of objects. In his words, the arts allow for a 'complete merging of playfulness with seriousness' (p. 279).

The integration of art and life, one of the central tenets of progressive education, struck a chord with artists and scholars who wanted education to encourage students' emotional as well as intellectual development. One educational experiment that was directly influenced by Dewey's ideas was Black Mountain College in North Carolina. Black Mountain College was founded in 1933 with the intention of providing a liberal learning environment in which university students and staff lived and worked together, with everyone sharing equally in domestic duties and the running of the college farm. In line with Dewey's arguments, the arts were central to this progressive education, and students were encouraged to experiment with forms of performance that framed everyday life, thereby illustrating how ordinary objects and sounds might be perceived as works of art. One particularly well-known example of this aesthetic ambition was a spontaneous performance which took place at Black Mountain College in 1952 and was later to inspire the 'Happenings' developed by Allan Kaprow in the United States and Albert Hunt in the United Kingdom in the 1960s. At the 1952

Untitled Event, the composer John Cage performed a 'composition with a radio' that used the everyday noises of the radio, the artist Robert Rauschenberg played old records on a hand-wound gramophone, the pianist David Tudor poured water from one bucket to another, and Charles Olson read his poetry. The creative focus for this event was not the performers but the spectators, who were required to make their own meanings from what they had witnessed. When Black Mountain College closed in 1957, it had already influenced a generation of neo-avant-garde artists, including Cage and choreographer Merce Cunningham. Dewey's theories of creativity and 'free expression' also inspired Winifred Ward, who founded the Creative Dramatics movement in the 1930s, and she applied them to children's artistic and personal development. Ward's Children's Theatre of Evanston advocated creative dramatics as a way of extending children's individual growth, and it also employed child actors with experience of improvisation and dramatic play on the basis that their acting technique had benefited from this training.

It was the social and egalitarian ambitions of progressive education that particularly appealed to those working in state schools in the United Kingdom, rather than its impact on children's acting or on neo-avant-garde art. The Second World War had interrupted the pace of educational change, but in the post-war era new teaching methods were sought that would erode class divisions. By the 1950s teaching methods inspired by both Deweyan theories of learning and child psychology were gradually finding their way into schools. The ideas of progressive educationalists such as Susan Isaacs, Christian Schiller and Molly Brearley gained status during the 1960s, becoming integrated into education policy with the publication of the Plowden Report, *Children and Their Primary Schools*, in 1967. Although it would be wrong to suggest that Dewey was the sole originator of progressive education, he can be justifiably credited with popularising the idea that children learn best by doing. This way of thinking about learning now seems familiar, but at the time active approaches to learning signified a move away from the rote learning that had dominated education until the 1960s.

If mainstream theatre was to have any place in the educational climate of the mid-twentieth century, it needed to be re-conceptualised to keep pace with the changes in teaching and learning pioneered by progressive educationalists. By the 1950s, suspicion towards the theatre had become widespread. As Dan Rebellato has pointed out in his study of British theatre *1956 and All That* (1999), growing mistrust of theatre was built on two apparently contradictory positions. On the one hand, theatre in London's West End was regarded as conformist and predictable, a shallow bourgeois confection dominated by the superficial glamour of the star system. On the other, this stereotype was matched by the homophobic suggestion that beneath this apparent respectability lay a hotbed of vice among actors, and that the theatre masked a homosexual subculture.

It is unsurprising, given this attitude to the theatre, that children were to be protected from its influence. The successful journal *Theatre in Education: A Bulletin of the Drama, in University, College, School or Youth Group* ran from 1947 to 1953 and contributed to the dissemination of educational principles and dramatic practices in four issues each year. (It is widely believed that the term 'theatre in education' was coined in the 1960s, but it is interesting to note that the expression was already well known and debated in the 1940s.) The remit of this journal included all kinds of theatre that took place in educational settings, including plays that toured to schools, children's theatre, youth theatre and drama in schools and universities. The first issue in 1947 set the tone for the journal's eclecticism by promising that it would address the following objectives:

1. The importance of the study of drama as a subject in the school curriculum
2. The value of practical dramatic activity as an educational medium. (p. 1)

The first objective, which involved young people visiting the theatre, was controversial, and there were fears that children would be tainted by acting and spoiled by the frivolity of theatrical spectacle. This warning, attributed to drama educator John Allen in the same 1947 issue, is perhaps typical of the concerns raised about presenting theatre to children:

> One of dangers in presenting plays to children
> is that their minds may become debauched with
> too much sensation and excitement. There must

be restraint in the extent to which one uses col-
our, music and so on. (p. 6)

The journal's second objective, to promote drama as an educational medium, was more readily embraced by theatre practitioners who were seeking to link new theatrical methods with progressive educational practices.

Teachers of drama and professional theatre-makers have long been in conversation with each other, and ideas and practices have frequently been shared across the two sectors. The rejection of the values of both commercial theatre and traditional education led directly to the establishment of a new form of theatre that quickly became known as Theatre-in-Education (TIE). This theatrical pedagogy sought to encourage young people to participate in theatre as a learning medium and as a vehicle for social change. Belgrade Theatre Coventry led the way by forming the first professional Theatre-in-Education company in 1965, with the explicit intention of devising working methods that were radically different from the conservative practices of mainstream theatre. Writing in Tony Jackson's edited collection *Learning through Theatre: Essays and Casebooks on Theatre in Education* (1980), David Pammenter, one of the founder members of Belgrade Coventry TIE, offers this explanation of the company's attitude to 'our' theatre, or, in other words, to the British theatre they witnessed at the time:

Much of our theatre has to do with sexual titilla-
tion of the worst order, it is nostalgic, backward-

> looking, and safe. It plays to a small percentage
> of the population which is, in the main, middle-
> class. The values it reflects, often reinforces and
> usually fails to explore, are usually middle-class
> values and assumptions. (p. 42)

Not only does this statement echo contemporary attitudes
to commercial theatre; it also offers an important insight
into the company's socialist principles. Many early TIE
practitioners were motivated by Marxist politics, and they
saw theatre as integral to the class struggle, a way of raising
the necessary social awareness to overthrow capitalism. As a
consequence, many TIE practitioners distanced themselves
from commercial theatre by roundly condemning it on the
grounds of its middle-class values and, by implication, its
lack of relevance to the lives of working-class children.
I suspect that this company would have found my spangly
production of *Cinderella* impossibly bourgeois; clearly they
would not have been in the market for fur coats or Mme
H. Lieberg's foundation garments. For these revolutionary
practitioners, bringing theatre into education required new
forms of representation and new theatrical languages.

It is important not to underestimate the passionate
atmosphere of the 1960s, as it provides the context for
understanding both the development of TIE and subsequent
theatre education practices. Politically, it was an era of pro-
test, in which supporters of the anti-Vietnam war movement, civil rights movement, gay rights, women's rights and
the campaign for nuclear disarmament made their voices

heard through direct action. This spirit of rebellion is symbolised by the *évenements* of May 1968 in Paris, where students and workers united in riots and a general strike. Less confrontationally, youth culture flourished, and the decade brought hippies, flower power, free festivals, free love and rock music. Theatrically, it was also a time to question the boundaries between art and life, theatre and revolution, dramatic action and social activism. Many of the first TIE practitioners were young men and women, part of the generation that turned against the austere lifestyle of their parents and embraced the new and socially committed youth culture. Inspired by this atmosphere of freedom and revolution, they argued that TIE was participatory, dynamic, collaborative, playful, pertinent to young people and politically radical. In their Annual Report in 1970, Belgrade Coventry TIE summarised their political reservations about the relevance of the theatre to young people and, in terms reminiscent of Dewey, expressed their interest in bringing together the arts, playfulness and the everyday:

> We do not aim to create the social habit of theatre – it [TIE] is an imaginative experience in its own right, an extension of the games children play in everyday life. (cited in O'Toole, *Theatre in Education*, 1976, p. 13)

By the end of the 1960s, a decade of intense social and educational change, TIE practitioners held a passionate and theorised commitment to breaking the authoritarian

structures of a traditional education by taking radical forms
of theatre into schools.

Activism and education:
the Theatre-in-Education movement

Any innovation is always built on the past – 'Nothing
arises from nothing,' as Bertolt Brecht famously said – and
although it was new in its form and working methods in the
1960s and 1970s, TIE belonged to a tradition of popular and
political theatres that had developed earlier in the twentieth
century. Theatre had been used as a tool of social and political mobilisation by the Workers' Theatre Movement of
the 1920s and 1930s, when groups of theatre activists had
performed plays with socialist messages in factories, pubs
and working men's clubs and on the street. The roots of
TIE, always British in origin, have been well documented
by Roger Wooster in *Contemporary Theatre in Education*
(2007) and Anthony Jackson in *Theatre, Education and the
Making of Meanings* (2007), both of whom draw attention
to the relationship between TIE and theatre movements
that regarded themselves as an 'alternative' to the mainstream theatre.

The Workers' Theatre Movement was an international
movement, committed to furthering the cause of Communism, with organisations in places as far apart as
Australia, the United States, Europe and Japan. The British
Workers' Theatre Movement was founded in 1926, inspired
by the Bolshevik Revolution in Russia. Ness Edwards, one
of the leaders of The Workers' Theatre, articulated the

relationship between theatre and the Marxist revolution in his manifesto of 1930:

> The workers' drama must have the workers' cause at its heart; it must be the battleground of new ideas; in this way it enters the workers' struggle for life, and becomes alive, pulsating with the battle of life. *It must be a source of energy. It must borrow social energy by dramatizing the social struggle; it will then supply energy to carry through the social struggle.* (p. 194, italics original)

Edwards' emphasis on activity and energy is important. Apathy and passivity were held to be responsible for maintaining the capitalist system; it was hoped that using the energy of theatre as a 'cultural weapon' would unite the workers in a common revolutionary cause.

The belief that a live and popular theatre has the potential to educate and inspire collective action was to motivate socialist theatre workers internationally. The Federal Theatre Project, founded in 1935 in the United States, is a good example of how popular theatre was used as a vehicle of political mobilisation. The Federal Theatre Project served five US cities and generated a lively programme of circus, vaudeville, puppet shows and other performances, including theatre for children, which dramatised contemporary social issues from the point of view of the political Left. It was particularly well known for its Living Newspapers, a form of theatre that derived from the Workers' Theatre

Movement and used a montage of performance techniques to represent and comment on the daily news. Such dynamic and politically charged approaches to theatre-making had an enduring influence on political and community-based theatre. The immediacy of form and popular style influenced early TIE practices and also had an impact on their contemporaries in activist theatre, including British companies such as Red Ladder, Gay Sweatshop and The General Will and the San Francisco Mime Troupe and Bread and Puppet Theatre in the United States, all of which played an active role in the counter-cultural movements of the 1960s and 1970s.

Traces of this theatre history can be recognised in early TIE practices, both in motivation and in methodology. Two inter-related ideas were particularly influential on the emergent TIE movement. First, 'involvement', 'participation', 'process' and 'activity' are crucial words in TIE, and there was general agreement that TIE's primary objective was to use theatre as a tool to explore ideas, feelings and values rather than to teach children how to put on plays. Second, taking theatre to the people had been a central tenet of the Workers' Theatre Movement, and working in schools rather than theatre buildings was a logical extension of this democratic principle. In a polemic written in 1933, Tom Thomas had famously called for a 'propertyless theatre for the propertyless class', a phrase he used to illustrate his commitment to developing an accessible socialist 'theatre of ideas' rather than a bourgeois 'theatre of illusion' (p. 89). In terms reminiscent of Thomas' propertyless and socially engaged theatre, Gordon Vallins ends his account of the foundation of the Belgrade Coventry Theatre-in-Education team, 'The Beginnings of TIE' (1980), with the following words:

> Here was theatre focusing attention, concentrating ideas with imagination and immediacy, encouraging thought and understanding within the community. Theatres as buildings are not in themselves important. But what is important is the vital communication between people of thoughts, feelings and ideas and response to the living situation. TIE, from the beginning, was designed to contribute to just that. (p. 44)

Acting was far less important than debating, and the illusion of theatre was thought to be a hindrance to young people's engagement with the ideas and 'real' situations set up in many TIE programmes. *Big Deal*, a programme devised by Julie Holledge, Libby Mason, Harry Miller and Mervyn Watson for Belgrade Coventry TIE (1980), illustrates the combination of community involvement and political activism TIE sought to promote. The programme examines, on the basis of painstaking research into the actual events, how a local community in London had been destroyed to make way for office buildings. The company visited the school twice, first to perform a play to inspire the children's sympathy for the displaced community and, on the second occasion, to hold debates about the local council's decision to evict this community from their homes.

Democratising the means of production, a central tenet of much counter-cultural theatre at the end of the 1960s, ensured that the values that informed the TIE companies' dramatic output were consonant with the company members' working conditions and daily lives. Open dialogue was promised both in the rehearsal room and within the company's organisational structure. This spirit of collaboration led practitioners to describe themselves as actor/teachers, a term that recognised their hybrid skills and varied backgrounds. Actor/teachers were certainly required to fulfil a number of responsibilities: they needed to be able to combine skills as researchers, devisers and performers with the ability to work constructively and collaboratively with children. Some had worked in theatre; others were trained teachers. Eileen Murphy, an actor/teacher with Bolton Octagon TIE, confidently asserted in her introduction to *Sweetie Pie* (1975) that these people were 'the most talented members of both professions', who had been 'driven by impossible conditions to drop out and pool their talents in an exciting new method of working' (p. 6).

This 'exciting new method of working' required actor/teachers to bring together professional knowledge from education and the theatre. Most TIE companies combined scripted or devised performance with young people's participation in the drama, and they called these participatory performances 'programmes' because, unlike theatre for children, they often involved the company making several visits to a school and integrating their work into the curriculum. In noting the difficulties of documenting elements of participation, Christine Redington comments in her introduction to *Six T.I.E Programmes* (1987) that 'in these workshops the pupils are able to explore, both intellectually and emotionally, the issues raised in the play' (p. v). She cites techniques such as hot-seating, in which pupils ask the characters questions, and depiction, where the action is frozen and the image is analysed. These techniques are similar to the methodology developed by Augusto Boal, an influential Brazilian director widely known for using participatory theatre with marginalised communities. Although Boal's first book, *Theatre of the Oppressed* (1979), added to the repertoire of techniques in use, it is significant that TIE actor/teachers had already developed their own workshop methodologies before encountering his practices.

Debates ensued about whether the work should be developed collectively, with all actor/teachers taking an equal share of administration, script writing, devising, designing and so on, or whether they should work collaboratively, with roles and responsibilities being differentiated. One interesting consequence of sharing the decision-making process, a practice enthusiastically adopted by theatre activists, was that it often resulted in internal debates. Eileen Murphy recalled how the process of devising *Sweetie Pie* (Bolton, 1972), a ground-breaking TIE programme for sixteen- to eighteen-year-olds that challenged sexism, caused bitter disputes within the company. In her introduction to the script Murphy described the suggestion that they might tackle this subject as 'explosive', not least because the company was, at the time, riddled with sexist attitudes towards its women members. Out of the many heated discussions in the rehearsal room there emerged, in Murphy's words, 'a strong commitment to the play and to the political line it was to embody' (p. 16). It is interesting to note that the actors' creative process was deeply implicated in changing the internal politics of the theatre company as well as the actor/teachers' everyday lives, and that this approach enabled them to develop a script that challenged attitudes within the wider community.

Performance methodologies and political controversies

The integration of scripted performance and children's participation was genuinely innovative, and TIE's working practices were documented, both as scripts and in a range of related publications. John O'Toole was the first to provide an educational rationale for the work, in *Theatre in Education* (1976); Tony Jackson's edited collection *Learning through Theatre* defined the field in 1980. These publications not only offered an intellectual framework for TIE; they also captured the voices and reflections of practitioners who had led its development. Christine Redington's full-length study *Can Theatre Teach?* (1983) reflected on the theories and practices that had informed the first TIE companies.

When we read the scripts and the reflections on practice, it is clear that TIE companies derived inspiration from the ideas of Bertolt Brecht. Brecht's epic theatre was designed to transform spectators from passive recipients of a consumer culture to critical thinkers who were aware of their own oppressions. The dramatic devices and structures in Brecht's work were, therefore, inseparable from the social and political function of theatre as he saw it. The *Lehrstücke*, translated by John Willett in *Brecht on Theatre: The Development of an Aesthetic* (1964) as 'learning plays', aimed to develop systems of learning that reflected socialist principles rather than bourgeois values. Brecht regarded the *Lehrstücke* as a rehearsal for a new society, and therefore the plays provided a dynamic way to represent 'the world as it changes' (p. 79). In terms of learning, Brecht claimed that the *Lehrstücke* treated audiences as 'a collection of individuals, capable of thinking and reasoning' rather than as a 'mob' that 'can be reached only through the emotions' (p. 79). Roswitha Mueller, in her essay 'Learning for a New Society: The *Lehrstück*' (1994), summarised the political purpose of the *Lehrstücke* thus:

> The *Lehre* itself, learned in practical exercises, is concerned with the acquisition of a number of attitudes – not specifically political decisions – that are necessary for a strategy towards a socialist society. Learning how to think dialectically is central and applies to the content just as much as it does to the formal arrangement. (p. 86)

The suggestion that theatre might be used to teach young people to think dialectically – to think, in other words, in ways that contradicted the dominant capitalist ideology – influenced TIE in both structure and form. Breaking the illusion associated with bourgeois theatre also involved, in the *Lehrstücke*, eroding hierarchical divisions between actors and audiences, and the performers added improvisation to an unfixed script. The *Lehrstücke* further matched the aspirations of TIE insofar as Brecht was interested in working outside theatre buildings and, significantly, advocated involving children and members of the community in the performance. At the premier of *Die Maßnahme* (*The Measures Taken*) in Berlin in 1930, for example, the role of the Controller was taken by a mass chorus of 3,000 workers. Working outside the confines of the proscenium arch theatre with a large 'cast' inevitably required radical approaches to staging and scenography.

A good example of the influence of Brecht's theatre, and of the *Lehrstücke* in particular, on TIE is a programme called *The Navigators*, which was devised for seven- and eight-year-olds by Belgrade Coventry TIE and published in 1980. This programme tells the story of the dangerous working conditions of the navigators (or 'navvies') who were employed to build the Kilsby railway tunnel near Coventry in the nineteenth century. The plot revolves around two central characters, Cat's Eyes Kilbride and First-Time O'Flynn. As navvies digging the railway tunnel, Kilbride and O'Flynn experience exploitation at the hands of Mr Lean, the contractor. The dramatic climax at the end of the programme comes when the children witness the two navvies in a life-threatening situation as they are forced to enter the tunnel to re-ignite a fuse to blast through the final section of rock. Throughout the programme the children are positioned as 'friends, fellow navvies' to these central characters; they are taught to use imaginary picks and shovels, to work inside the dangerous tunnel. Through the embodiment of these roles, the children are asked to identify with the predicament of the navvies as they face unemployment, poverty and physical danger.

Core to the dramatic composition of *The Navigators* is the negotiation between documentary and commentary, a central feature of Brecht's *Lehrstücke*. This device enables the actors to break the Aristotelian unities of time, place and action and focuses attention on how the dramatic situation might be both experienced and read. One instance of this dynamic negotiation between documentary and commentary, or action and reflection, comes after Kilbride has led the children, in role as navvies, in the communal singing of a work song:

> O'Flynn: I've come down here to work on this tunnel. What? You're going to be working there as well. Have you met the contractor? Do you know if he wants any gangers?
>
> Kilbride: Aye, he wants two.
>
> O'Flynn: Well what are we sitting round here for talking – Cat's Eyes you sort out these navvies and I'll get my gear.
>
> Kilbride: And that's where my story goes on from, because I'd sat round here most of the day waiting for First-Time to turn up. (p. 69)

This sequence of documentary dialogue and commentary is in part a device to move the plot forward. But it also encourages the children to position themselves alongside the navvies, who are warm, humorous and sympathetic characters, and to distance themselves from the capitalist Mr Lean, who is presented as a recognisable Victorian stereotype with top hat and cane. The commentary frames the action, enabling the children to observe the situation from both inside and outside the dramatic action. This dialectic, a process of action and reflection, ensures that the class of seven- and eight-year-olds are inevitably led to sympathise with the struggles of the working class.

There is an energy about *The Navigators* that is generated by the combination of lively characterisation and well-researched local history. Published collections of TIE programmes edited by Pam Schweitzer (1980) and Christine Redington (1987) include works by Belgrade Coventry, Greenwich Young People's Theatre, Bolton Octagon, Leeds TIE, Action Pie in Cardiff, Pit Prop in Wigan and Lancaster TIE that make use of similar dramaturgical devices. Programmes were tightly structured to allow young people to participate, and the use of naturalistic dialogue, direct address and clear exposition of plot enabled the actor/teachers to move seamlessly from performance to facilitation. Not only did this avoid what Brecht regarded as the seduction of the theatrical spectacle; the dramatic form encouraged young people to enter the action without feeling self-conscious or that they had to 'act'. As in the *Lehrstücke*, the methodology of TIE was inseparable from its social and educational function, and the participatory performance of TIE marked a significant development of Brecht's unfinished cultural project.

Good theatre is not, of course, bland and uncontroversial. It challenges and inspires, and it was this element that led some TIE companies to clash with the authorities. In the introduction to *Six T.I.E Programmes*, Redington comments that because TIE 'deals with socio-political subjects' companies became open to political censorship (p. v). Some companies, moreover, became increasingly vulnerable to charges of political indoctrination. This was in part due to the dramatic form they used: although Brecht's *Lehrstück* has the potential to encourage dialectical thought, it has also been read as an instrument of manipulation. The documentary structure and use of direct address, it is argued, can militate against interpretations that do not follow the performers' political beliefs. Some educational authorities saw this use of dramatic form, along with the programmes' content, as provocative.

The TIE programme *Questions Arising in 1985 from a Mutiny in 1789* (Cardiff, 1985), devised by Action Pie, became the subject of particular controversy. The director, Geoff Gillham, was a prominent TIE practitioner who later directed the British premieres of Edward Bond's plays for young people, including *Eleven Vests* (1997) and *At the Inland Sea* (1995). An active supporter of the British miners' strike in 1985, Gillham explicitly cited Brecht to justify the parallels between this strike and the mutiny on the *Bounty* in 1789. In his introduction to the published version of the play,

Gillham's vocabulary is unequivocally Brechtian: he claimed that theatre should be treated as a rational, scientific process and that, as such, it should lead young people to understand 'the objective laws of human behaviour as they pertain (in this case) to how people come to rebellion' (p. 92). The play's dramatic action is interrupted, in the manner of the *Lehrstücke*, by the narrator, whose simple and unambiguous Marxist statements comment on the dramatic situation:

> For a long time, people live under conditions
>   they should not tolerate.
> It is not that they *do* accept them:
> But that they do not know they have the power
>   to change them. (p. 97)

Increasingly didactic declarations punctuate the play, culminating in this final rhetorical question:

> When the oppressed rise up and seize the power.
> They're always confronted with the clash
>   between wishes and necessity.
> But that's in the way of things; that's what
>   power's about.
> So who is more fit to wield it?
> The oppressed or the oppressor. (p. 113)

This overt political commentary seems to make the audience complicit in the play's politics. However, Gillham recorded that in performance some adults resented this intervention, protesting that they 'didn't like being told what to think'

(p. 91). In his defence, he invoked the work of both Brecht and drama-in-educationalist Dorothy Heathcote to support his argument that 'our job as artists is to struggle to understand it [the world] and then to create a sensuous representation of it, which enables others (the pupils) to understand it' (p. 91). Gillham suggested that young people found similarities between the captain who oppresses the crew on the *Bounty* and authoritarian headteachers, so that the programme had relevance to their everyday lives. Whether this was a blatant use of theatre to indoctrinate young people into revolutionary politics or a legitimate application of theatre to address inequality rather depends on your point of view. Certainly, following this controversial production, Action Pie had its public funding withdrawn. So, what had changed?

Transitions and tensions

One of the central arguments of this book is that the application of professional theatre to educational contexts is always dependent on the social, cultural and political climates in which it takes place. This was certainly the case with the TIE movement, as it explicitly sought to engage with the social issues of the day. The optimism that characterised the 1960s and 1970s began to wane, however, and a number of changes took place during the 1980s and 1990s that had significant repercussions for TIE and other forms of educational theatre. The election of the Right-wing Conservative prime minister Margaret Thatcher in 1979 in the United Kingdom and Ronald Reagan's election as president shortly afterwards in 1981 in the United States marked the end of an era for the political Left.

Perhaps most significant to theatre-makers who had built their practice on socialist principles was that the changing socio-political climate in the 1980s was accompanied by a crisis in the political Left. The fall of the Berlin Wall in 1989 symbolised the end of the cold war that had existed between the capitalist West and the Communist Soviet Union since the 1940s, and the subsequent demise of Communism meant that the Marxist narratives and principles that many educational theatre-makers had lived by were plunged into uncertainty. Put simply, there seemed little point in starting a revolution to overthrow capitalism when Communism had already collapsed.

On a practical level, as the traditional landmarks of politics were re-negotiated during the 1980s and early 1990s, the function of education and the social role of theatre were once again subject to critical review. In education, this period was characterised by a call to return to the 'basics' of traditional teaching methods after decades of what the political Right regarded as the failures of progressive and child-centred education. Obviously this meant that TIE, which was based on experiential learning, came under fire. As times became increasingly uncertain, internal tensions within the TIE movement began to show, and differences in attitudes became increasingly entrenched. At its most harmonious, the movement had constructively integrated the Marxist aesthetics of Brecht's theatre with liberal theories of progressive education to create a convincing rationale for the participatory methodologies of TIE. But, when challenged, the movement became polarised between orthodox Marxists who argued that TIE was a means of politicisation and liberal educationalists whose more politically pliable child-centred philosophies led them to adapt to changes in the school curriculum.

British TIE was particularly affected by the political crisis that engulfed the Left. Elsewhere in the world TIE had never secured the same popularity as in the United Kingdom. The length of programmes, poor production values and expense were variously blamed for its lack of international success, but not, interestingly, its political orientation. Australian TIE, which had been influenced by the British tradition in its early days, had never really taken hold; as O'Toole and Bundy point out in 'Kites and Magpies: TIE in Australia' (1993), there was no great appetite for participatory theatre in Australian schools. In his essay 'Theatre in Education: Dead or Alive?' (1998), Geoffrey Milne states that by the late 1980s many Australian Theatre-in-Education companies had been replaced by youth theatres or professional theatre companies that toured shows to school audiences. Some interest in TIE had been generated in the United States, particularly by the Creative Arts Team in New York, but the less ideologically driven Theatre for Children had dominated theatre provision for young people.

The British situation is significant not only because it casts light on the pressures on both education and theatre at the time but also because this history paved the way for much theatre education in the twenty-first century. Of the many accounts of the decline of TIE in UK schools, I have chosen to use as my guide the analysis offered by Nicolas Whybrow in 'Young People's Theatre and the New Ideology of State Education' (1994). By 1994 it was possible to see the longer-term effects of the Conservative Party's policies on TIE, as cuts in public funding had taken serious hold. Whybrow points out that TIE companies had, historically, served their local schools and that they were therefore often funded by the local education authority (LEA). When the Thatcher government withdrew funding from the LEAs, and under-funded schools were expected to manage their own budgets, even the most supportive LEAs were forced to make cuts to the funding of their local TIE companies. From 1993 to 1994, Belgrade Coventry TIE experienced a cut of £30,000, leading to redundancies and a requirement that, in return for the reduced funding it did receive, the company's artistic and educational policies would be subject to scrutiny from LEA officials. Writing about the situation in 1994, Whybrow notes that this was 'a procedure that is rapidly becoming familiar to TIE companies associated with cash-strapped regional theatres' (p. 199).

Equally significantly, and perhaps more pertinent to the development of theatre and education in the twenty-first century, were changes to the ways in which drama was taught in schools. In many parts of the world the curriculum became increasingly compartmentalised: the National Curriculum for England and Wales was introduced in 1988 with the explicit intention of promoting more subject-centred teaching. TIE encouraged learning *through* theatre, and this relied on a school curriculum that was sufficiently flexible to allow for interdisciplinary approaches to learning. A good TIE programme could provide a catalyst for several weeks' work, particularly in primary schools, that might include history, geography, art, science and creative writing. An increasingly prescriptive curriculum meant that there was less flexibility to integrate different subjects in this way. In secondary schools drama was gaining popularity as an optional examination subject in the fourteen to eighteen age range, and, after the expansion of university drama departments during the 1970s, there were increasing numbers of graduates with degrees in drama entering the teaching profession who welcomed the opportunity to teach at examination level. Although syllabuses encouraged improvisation and students were expected to respond to dramatic situations in role, they were also asked to develop devising skills, work practically on plays and gain knowledge and understanding of practitioners such as Brecht and Stanislavski.

The place of drama in the curriculum was hotly contested during the 1980s and 1990s. In his book *Education and Dramatic Art* (1989), David Hornbrook challenged the orthodoxies of drama-in-education, arguing that its roots in progressive education and its emphasis on spontaneous improvisation militated against young people learning about theatre as an art form. This meant, in his view, that generations of young people were culturally disenfranchised. Hornbrook's argument was based on a cultural materialist analysis of society and drew heavily on Marxist social theory, but it is interesting that, in the educational climate of the time, his work was read as endorsing the élitism of mainstream theatre and encouraging politically conservative teaching methods. This reading was exacerbated by the fact that part of Hornbrook's criticism of drama-in-education was directed towards Gavin Bolton and Dorothy Heathcote, who, as international pioneers in movement, were held in much affection and esteem. Gavin Bolton's book *Acting in Classroom Drama* (1998) clarified his position. He argued that approaches to learning that involve both children and teachers taking roles in an unfolding drama (major methodologies of drama-in-education) are inherently theatrical, requiring the participants to adopt 'acting behaviours' (p. 249).

Alongside cuts in funding, the location of TIE in the arts curriculum signalled its decline. TIE had been, historically, opposed to teaching children about theatre-making, and so there was some resentment about young people using the experience of TIE to understand theatre form. Whybrow notes that the introduction of drama at examination level had led to 'the increasingly misapplication of companies' work, with students being told by teachers to take notes about its formal aspects – set design, acting style, and so on' (p. 274). This suggests a mismatch between the school curriculum and TIE. It also rehearses the assumption, widely held at the time, that consideration of the formal or craft elements of performance precluded young people's emotional or intellectual engagement with the content of the programme, or, as Whybrow puts it, with 'unpredictable and controversial factors which creative learning about life issues implies' (p. 274).

My own experience as a secondary school drama teacher is perhaps relevant here, as it illuminates some of the issues faced by teachers during this period. I wanted to maintain a long-standing commitment to raising serious and controversial questions through drama, as well as to encouraging students to become active theatre-makers for themselves. For me, these two objectives were not mutually exclusive, particularly when supported by thought-provoking and innovative professional theatre. Although some excellent TIE was produced during this period, once funding for local companies had been cut the quality of work offered to schools became increasingly unreliable. I regularly received adverts from young actors who were using TIE as a stepping-stone to careers in mainstream theatre and whose one-off visits to schools (known somewhat uncharitably as 'flash and dash') simply repeated a formula rather than experimenting with new ways of working. Without the political and educational commitment that characterised the best work, TIE gradually shifted from a movement to a theatrical genre, and it became synonymous with well-known patterns and repetitive methodologies. Given a limited budget, this was a serious consideration for drama teachers. My own response, as head of an arts faculty, was not untypical: we would continue to work closely with local TIE companies whose work we valued (we had a good relationship with a company called Public Parts, led by Tim Crouch), but we would also develop links with the local theatre, in my case Bristol

Old Vic Theatre, which, in return for government funding for its main house productions, was expected to develop
an education programme. I served on a steering group that
discussed the theatre's programming, and this led to some
exciting productions that appealed to young people. I vividly remember taking students to see Athol Fugard's *Master
Harold and the Boys* (Bristol Old Vic Theatre, 1990). This
was one of Matthew Warchus' first productions as a director, and he generously gave my students time to discuss his
interpretations and ways of working, an opportunity that
had a profound effect on them. Many had little knowledge
of Apartheid South Africa, and the experience led them to
devise their own performance to deepen their understanding of this social injustice.

In his essay 'Theatre in Education: What Remains?'
(1994) Whybrow, in common with many advocates of TIE
at the time, rehearsed the argument that an education in
theatre 'runs the risk of giving rise to different forms of
élitist (class-based) stigmatisation' (p. 277). Although this
was a serious consideration, many drama teachers recognised that not all theatre promoted middle-class values and
understood that, taught imaginatively, a diversity of theatre
practices could provide a rich resource for young people's
learning. In some ways the need for high-quality theatre for
children and young people had been acknowledged in the
United States and Australia much earlier, but its educational
purpose had not been fully articulated and theorised at the
time. Some emergent Australian playwrights, as O'Toole
and Bundy point out in 'Kites and Magpies', were able to

hone their craft by writing educational plays. The challenge that faced theatre educators in the 1990s, which remains relevant today, is how to maintain the educational purpose and commitment that characterised the most innovative TIE and at the same time redefine its aesthetics and politics for a new cultural and educational climate.

Beyond Theatre-in-Education

Theatre, when it meets education, often articulates deeply felt social aspirations as well as giving shape and form to the circumstances and difficulties faced by young people in the here-and-now. One enduring legacy of TIE practitioners is that they showed how to develop a theatrical pedagogy by asking profound questions about the purpose of education, the social role of theatre and its ability to affect the lives of young people. So, to continue that spirit of inquiry, what are the most important questions to raise about the role of theatre now? What contribution might theatre make to education in the twenty-first century? Is there still a place for live theatre in a world that is saturated by digital technologies? How might theatre affect the lives of young people today?

Young people living in the twenty-first century are often complexly positioned between different emotional attachments, beliefs and value systems; their access to instant social networks, multiple sources of information and mediated images means that growing up with a confident sense of selfhood and citizenship, always a troubling process, is fraught with new uncertainties. The theatre director John

Retallack, whose Company of Angels was founded in 2001 with the explicit aim of making innovative theatre for and with young people, observed in his book *Company of Angels* (2007) that it is often young people who 'experience social change in the most direct and brutal way' (p. 10). The contribution that professional theatre-makers can make to the education of young people within this cultural landscape has become increasingly difficult to define, not least because there are so many competing and sometimes conflicting pressures on young people themselves and on how their futures might be shaped.

Questions about the social role of theatre at the beginning of the twenty-first century have focused on its immediacy and liveness. One argument is that theatre is, by its very nature, live, local and public, and therefore has the potential to disrupt the homogenising tendencies associated with globalisation. Baz Kershaw has argued that globalisation is sustained by carefully managed performances of power, by which he means that the fabric of society in the affluent West has become regulated by many different forms of non-theatrical 'performance'. Elements of performance have permeated many areas of life, including performance management in the workplace, where targets are set and employees expected to 'perform' well enough to meet them, the performance of slick sound-bites from politicians and the careful staging of world events by the media. This is perhaps particularly obvious during elections, when candidates' carefully manufactured films designed to show them as 'real people' often show 'ordinary people' and are underscored by soft music. In the 2008 US election, for example, both Barack Obama and John McCain published videos on YouTube that had been staged to combine approachability with statesmanship. In *Theatre Ecologies: Environment and Performance Events* (2007), Kershaw calls these 'performative societies', in which 'every dimension of human exchange and experience is suffused by performance and gains a theatrical quality' (p. 12). Young people growing up in performative societies inevitably absorb the imagery they see, and, it is argued, their imaginations are influenced by a highly commodified culture industry. One of the challenges of theatre, therefore, is to interrogate how performances of power have been constructed and find different ways to imagine and symbolise experience.

Contemporary theatre education is undergoing a period of transformation both artistically and politically. Artistically, a new generation of drama and theatre educators have been inspired both by the reflexivity and spontaneity of drama education methodologies and by a re-energised professional theatre and performance culture. New paradigms of theatre and performance have proliferated in response to twenty-first-century circumstances, and these new performance vocabularies are filtering into education. Theatre education has, therefore, extended its dramatic repertoire from a prevalence of naturalistic theatre that relied on dialectical thought to interrogate social issues, and it now includes a wide range of performance styles that push the boundaries of representation, such as site-specific performance, live art, installation and autobiographical performance, all of which are found at the cutting edge of contemporary theatre-making. Politically, there is no longer one single ideology or clearly identifiable narrative that unites theatre-makers who work in education, and this means that there are multiple reasons for bringing theatre into education. In this climate of uncertainty, however, young people are finding a place to develop with professional theatre-makers theatrical languages and performance vocabularies that reflect their identities and represent their experiences in an increasingly globalised and mediatised world.

In an attempt to shed some light on how theatre education is responding to the challenges of living in the twenty-first century, I have chosen, for the remainder of this book, to select three inter-related themes. First, I revisit the concept of the imagination and raise questions about the social efficacy of theatre. Second, I explore questions of place, in part because gaining a secure sense of identity and belonging has become increasingly problematic for many young people living in a globalised world. Finally, I question the role of creativity in twenty-first-century education, asking how theatre might maintain its traditional position as cultural provocateur in an educational context in which creativity is regarded as an economic necessity. These questions are, of course, highly selective and by no means exhaustive, but they are intended to prompt some thinking about how contemporary practices are responding to new circumstances.

Changing performance methodologies mean that there are also tricky issues of terminology to address. Practitioners who work in educational contexts today tend to use terms such as 'theatre education', 'theatre in education', 'creative learning', 'educational theatre' and 'theatre as education' rather flexibly and interchangeably, so, to indicate the cross-over between different forms of theatre and education, from now on I refer to all practices generically as 'theatre education' unless there is a specific reason to define the terms more explicitly. Perhaps most pertinently, this indicates that a new generation of theatre-makers are eroding old divisions between theatre as an art form and theatre as a learning medium, between theatre-in-education and the theatre, between play and art.

The battle for the imagination

Connections between theatre and the imagination are deeply felt and widely held, although the social role the imagination plays in theatre-making has been re-conceptualised over time. The playwrights Edward Bond and Howard Barker hold, as I suggested earlier, very different views about theatre-in-education, but they share a belief that the theatre has the potential to disturb and enrich the imagination. Edward Bond's view, expressed in 'Notes on Theatre-in-Education', that the future 'depends on the state of our imaginations' (p. 58) emphasises the social and political role of the imagination, whereas in *Arguments for a Theatre*, Barker regards theatre as being 'like children's play' and suggests that, as such, imaginative theatre is 'world-inventing' (p. 75).

Writing about the effects of the performative society on theatre, the Scottish playwright David Greig argues that the imagination is increasingly managed in this new globalised, interconnected world. He suggests that the carefully constructed images and narratives through which the world's news is presented shield people from empathetic responses to those who are experiencing injustice. Greig cites Sarah Kane's play *Blasted* (Royal Court, London, 1995) to illustrate the social efficacy of the imagination and to argue that theatre can ask audiences to imagine the unimaginable. In his essay 'Rough Theatre' (2008), Greig argues that *Blasted* insists that audiences empathise with those caught up in the war in Bosnia; the play demands that they consider what would it would be like to experience the violent 'hell and bloodshed' of the Bosnian war first-hand (p. 219). Kane neither analysed nor represented Bosnia in the play, Greig suggests; she *imagined* it, and in so doing she confronted audiences with the immediacy and horror of a war that seemed distant and remote when received through the mediated images of television news. Referring to his own role as a playwright, Greig describes the political significance of the imagination in contemporary theatre:

> Theatre doesn't change the world. I have no illusions that a play of mine will lead to mass demonstrations or the overthrow of governments. However, I do believe that if the battleground is the imagination, then the theatre is a very appropriate weapon in the armoury of resistance. (p. 219)

Rather than seeking dialectical solutions to contemporary social issues, a practice he associates with '1970s left-wing dinosaurs', Greig argues for a new model of political theatre that is 'rough', immediate and 'unfinished'. In an era of globalisation, Greig argues, the theatre offers a place to open up 'the multiple possibilities of the imagination' (p. 212).

The social imaginary of live theatre, Greig argues, enables audiences and theatre-makers to empathise and reflect, to question and unfix packaged, second-hand and commodified images of the world. If this is the case, and the contemporary battle ground is the imagination, professional theatre-makers have a significant contribution to make to education. It is in this context that I should like to apply to contemporary practice the theoretical insights of the philosopher Paul Ricoeur in order to question how the imagination might be understood. I am interested in whether a reading of the social imaginary developed by Ricoeur can help my analysis of twenty-first-century theatre education. What is particularly interesting about Ricoeur's work, and why it seems relevant to theatre education, is not that theatre-makers have been directly informed by reading his work but that it offers a way of thinking about how the imagination is used both to maintain and to question the ideological structures and values of society.

In his study of the social imaginary, *Lectures on Ideology and Utopia* (1986), Ricoeur argues that one function of the imagination is to 'preserve and order' specific ideologies or narratives by perpetuating images and stories that represent the dominant tradition of a culture or society. Conversely, he argues, the imagination can also have a 'disruptive function' that will 'help us to re-think the nature of our social life' (p. 266). The disruptive imagination is utopian, according to Ricoeur, because imagining the world to be different breaks the assumption that there is inevitably a shared, 'common sense' ideological position around which everyone can or should unite. Social change can come about only, in Ricoeur's view, when these two different and contrasting functions of the imagination are brought together. A productive imagination can emerge when the utopian imagination that looks forward to create the future is in dialogue with the ideological symbols of the past: 'Ideology as a symbolic confirmation of the past and utopia as a symbolic opening towards the future are complementary' (p. 30). In this context, the task of the creative imagination is to further a new social imaginary by asking questions about the ideological meanings of the symbols, histories, celebrations, rituals and other forms of theatrical and non-theatrical performance that sustain contemporary society, and by using the insights gained to imagine new possibilities.

Ricoeur's social imaginary suggests that there is a continued role for theatre-makers as cultural critics, both in education and in the theatre. It is in this context that a renewed case can be made for introducing theatricality into education. Josette Féral, in her introduction to a special issue of the journal *Substance* dedicated to theatricality (2002), provides a succinct description of the term:

> It [theatricality] creates disjuncture where our
> ordinary perception sees only unity between

signs and their meanings. It replaces uniformity with duality. It perceives the friction and tensions between the various worlds it observes, and obliges us to see differently. (p. 11)

This description of theatricality is reminiscent of Ricoeur's disruptive utopian imagination; it creates a 'gap', Féral argues, 'between everyday space and representational space, between reality and fiction', and it is this gap that 'obliges us to see differently' (p. 11). Crucially, because the gap between fiction and reality needs to be filled by the imaginations of artists and audiences, this also recognises that there is no straightforward or easy elision between participation in drama and political or personal empowerment. As Ricoeur convincingly argued, the imagination is not in itself morally good or benign; it can serve many different values, ideologies and belief systems.

Linked to theatricality and applied to education, a re-defined social imagination enables young people to raise critical questions about the performative society in which they live and invites them to imagine that which was previously unimagined or unimaginable. In a cultural climate that is mediated and represented by global capitalism, it is the unpredictable qualities of live theatre that have the potential to extend young people's horizons beyond the familiar, to disrupt the everyday and the conventional. This is theatre that, in Barker's terms, 'invents life' and, in Edward Bond's dramatic pedagogy, enables children to 'bear witness to life'.

The process of imagining

Theatricality is an imaginative process rather than a particular quality or aesthetic product; thus, in relation to theatre education, there are many ways in which it might inform practice. Although it would be wrong to imply that TIE does not sometimes still exist in its classic form, a significant and recent addition to theatre education provision is the development of education programmes in mainstream theatres. With support from the technical and human resources that are housed in theatres, many of these programmes attempt to balance the social imaginary of theatre with learning about theatre craft or, to evoke Brecht, to find connections between the theatre of illusion and the theatre of ideas.

Writing about such education programmes in *The Young Vic Book: Theatre Work and Play* (2004), Ruth Little observed:

> The perspective shift that has accompanied the new approach is based on the recognition that young people are as interested in the mysteries and mechanics of making and presenting theatre as they are in the ideas and issues that plays explore. (p. 18)

The National Theatre in London has been influential in encouraging young people's understanding of theatre-making through its *Connections* scheme. This scheme has commissioned new plays by established playwrights such as Mark Ravenhill, Sarah Daniels, Enda Walsh, Winsome

Pinnock and Maya Chowdhry for young people to perform, often with the support of professional theatre-makers. None of the plays is explicitly written to address contemporary 'issues' in any didactic sense, but each is careful to raise important social questions for young people to explore. Mark Ravenhill's ironically titled *Citizenship* (National Theatre, London, 2005), for example, offers a comic analysis of young people's struggle for recognition and invites young actors to confront attitudes to sexuality. From one point of view, working in theatre buildings risks a return to the seduction of theatre that was so criticised by the TIE movement. Looked at differently, however, the illusion of theatre can be broken when young people learn to make it for themselves, and particularly when they are encouraged to work on productions and scripts that provide creative and intellectual challenges.

In Féral's terms, finding points of connection between the fictional world created by a playwright and lived experience is integral to realising the script's theatricality. Following Deweyan principles of experiential learning, the process of rehearsal can encourage young people to engage imaginatively with new ideas and unfamiliar forms of representation. A script is not, of course, a fixed blueprint for performance but a starting-point for another set of interpretations, and the 'gap' between page and stage needs to be filled by the imagination. In other words, by working creatively with a script, young people have the opportunity to explore the differences and similarities between their own understanding of the world and the playwright's dramatic representation of ideas. They need to understand how theatrical symbols and codes make meaning, and how these codes can be interpreted and disrupted. Ricoeur's ideas again provide a helpful way to analyse the process of interpretation. In Ricoeur's terms, an active process of interpretation involves a 'poetics' of imagining, in which metaphor, symbol and narrative create an 'image-fiction' that is utopian and resistant to conservative or reactionary patterns of thought. Its opposite, Ricoeur suggests, is an 'image-picture' that has no critical or creative dimension and simply reproduces life as it is already known.

One particularly interesting example of a project that captured the utopian 'image-fiction' of theatre was the first production of Edward Bond's play *The Children*. The play was commissioned by Classworks Theatre Company in Cambridge, directed by Claudette Bryanston and performed at the Manor Community College in 2000 by two professional actors and a cast of young people from the school. I had the good fortune to work with the young cast before the rehearsal period and to research the process, which I later wrote about in 'Acting, Creativity and Justice: An Analysis of Edward Bond's *The Children*' (2003). The play asked what would have happened if Medea's children had been able to speak. *Medea*, a play by the ancient Greek playwright Euripides, tells the story of a woman who takes revenge for her husband's adultery by killing their children. Bond's plot draws contemporary parallels with Euripides' play by following a group of children (the Friends) on a journey in which they are systematically abused, betrayed and ultimately murdered by the adults they trust. The complexity of the play is represented in Bond's portrayal of the Mother, whose limitations make her pitiable rather than evil, a woman who is a victim of an unjust society. By placing the Friends in an extreme situation, Bond invited the young people in the cast to ask fundamental questions about how they would react in circumstances that were almost beyond their imaginations and, in the process, to consider who they were and who they would like to become.

In his essay 'Belgrade TIE' (1998), Bond argues that the 'imagination cannot be taught – but it can be made creative' (p. 119). *The Children* is a script that, if not unfinished, was open for the young people to improvise dialogue from within the structure and form of the play. This not only enabled them to explore the script in ways that had resonance for them; it also had the effect of valuing their voices, ideas and creative suggestions during the rehearsal period. When I interviewed Bond in 2000, he expressed the hope that the process of improvisation would enable the young people to relate to the dramatic situation, thereby making it 'real to the imagination'. I leant from the cast that playing fictional roles led them to imagine extreme risk and danger in a very immediate and embodied way. When I interviewed Karmen Fowell, a girl who played one of the Friends, she made clear connections between the imaginary world of the play, the character she played and the wider social world:

> I go off stage, and I know I'm dead. And I'm standing there thinking ... does anyone know I am dead?

> And then I'm thinking ... This could happen. It does
> happen. There's a girl, right, in the papers ... and
> she just goes away ... and no one notices for a bit
> and then they find out she's dead.

In reflecting on the first performance, Bond commented on the special presence the young people brought to the stage: '[T]hese young people were *there* because their imagination was fully there.' Performing the play had enabled the young people to engage with it on different levels; they identified intimately with the roles they played, and, in so doing, they were able to address wider questions about social isolation and social justice.

It is interesting that Bond describes his educational work as Theatre-in-Education rather than theatre for children or young people. This terminology not only invokes his well-documented allegiance to the socialist principles of the TIE movement; it also underlines his commitment to applying his plays to the process of education rather than the more commercial enterprise of children's theatre. It is also striking that many interesting contemporary plays or devised performances have been developed by those with a specialist understanding of both theatre and education, whether they are working in education departments of theatres or in companies that know how children learn. The London-based company Oily Cart, for example, specialises in making beautiful, multisensory and interactive theatre for the under-fives and for children with complex disabilities, and its work illustrates a deep understanding of its audiences.

Glasgow TAG Theatre Company, which emerged from the traditions of TIE and is part of Glasgow Citizens' Theatre, regularly commissions new plays and curates education projects that address social questions. David Greig's play about the rights of the child, *Dr Korczak's Example* (Citizens' Theatre, Glasgow, 2001), was written as part of TAG's *Making the Nation* project, which explored questions of citizenship and democracy. Following the practices of TIE, many subsidised theatres have fostered close links between local artists, playwrights and teachers, leading to sustained collaborations that are designed to support children's creative, cultural and social education.

Theatre for children has yet to achieve the same educational status as children's fiction or poetry and, thus, sometimes has an ambiguous position in relation to education. Specialist theatres for children, such as the Unicorn Theatre in London, The Ark in Dublin and the New Victory Theatre in New York, not only recognise that children are profitable cultural consumers but also run well-supported education programmes. These programmes vary in emphasis, but they usually include workshops that enhance children's experiences of attending performances as well as contributing to their arts education. The Unicorn Theatre's education provision complements its inventive theatre programme; it offers in-service training for teachers, post-show discussions, workshops about current productions and an opportunity for local children to perform their own work in the theatre at an annual festival. The New Victory's education programme is more family oriented, and the workshops offered promise to teach the whole family theatre skills such as clowning or puppetry. Research conducted at the University of Texas in 2006 revealed, however, that the commercial theatre for children in the United States is dominated by adaptations of popular novels and familiar stories, suggesting relatively unadventurous audiences and a fairly limited view of education (Dawson *et al.*, 2008). Although successful playwrights such as Susan Zeder and Aurand Harris have written challenging new plays for young people, it is difficult to find their work in repertoire in the United States. Notwithstanding that there is some very exciting and challenging work in children's theatre, when funding is short term or unreliable it can be difficult to achieve both innovative theatre and an imaginative education programme.

Of course, there is no guarantee that engaging with theatre, either as performers or audiences, will provide thought-provoking learning environments for young people; it is possible that such engagements will be used simply to promote what Bond describes, somewhat disparagingly, as saleable skills or to re-enforce a celebrity culture. Creating, in Ricoeur's terms, a utopian 'poetics' of imagining within theatre education requires favourable circumstances within the theatre as a cultural institution as well as theatre-makers able to inspire young people. The process of working theatrically can, however, provide young people with the critical and creative tools to interpret the performative society in which they live and can offer imaginative insights into another world which, once seen, cannot be unseen. 'Theatre cannot change the world,' as David Greig wrote in 'Rough Theatre', 'but it can offer a moment of liberated space through which we can change ourselves' (p. 220).

The social imaginary of place

The ideal of theatre as 'liberated space' needs to be set in the context of debates about the social meanings of theatres as places. One debate that has straddled the twentieth and twenty-first centuries articulates how the theatre, as both a place and a space, is experienced and understood. The idea of a propertyless theatre, a central political principle in the Workers' Theatre Movement, found renewed articulations in the TIE movement, as I have already described, when the democratic ambition to bring theatre closer to the people involved companies working in schools and other educational institutions rather than in theatre buildings. Although this was obviously one practical way in which whole classes could participate, the decision was also, of course, based on the perception that theatres as places represented cultural privilege and class division. This aspiration to make theatre education as socially inclusive as possible continues to inform much contemporary practice. Seen in this light, opening the doors of theatre buildings to young people not only provides access to different artistic practices; it is also a symbolic gesture designed to counter some of the more prejudicial meanings associated with the theatre as a cultural institution. Creating any kind of 'liberated space' in theatre, wherever it takes place, requires, therefore, an understanding of the politics of place.

The conceptual differences between how space and place have been understood are relevant here. Space, as an abstract concept, has been associated with movement, energy and freedom and has sometimes been perceived as a threat. When Peter Brook famously argued that theatre-making could happen in any 'empty space', he meant to imply a kind of liberated openness in which artistic practice is unconstrained by institutional structures. Place, in contrast, suggests the messiness and materiality of life, implying emotional attachments, allegiances and particular physical environments. In his book *Space and Place: The Perspective of Experience* (1977), Yi-Fu Tuan makes the following observation:

> What begins as undifferentiated space becomes place when we get to know it better and endow it with value. ... The ideas of 'space' and 'place' require each other for definition. From the security and stability of place we are aware of. the openness, freedom, and threat of space, and vice versa. (p. 7)

An anecdote might illustrate how, when spaces acquire meaning, they become places. A friend once took me to the town in which he grew up, and the stories he told about the places we visited – the route of his paper round, his school, the pub his father frequented, the station roof he climbed on to smoke his first illicit cigarettes – changed my understanding of this rather anonymous town. It became inscribed with new meanings, an intimate connection with the past. What this story also illustrates, however, is that a space is never empty; it always carries social connotations and it is always someone else's place.

In his book *The Production of Space* (1991), the French theorist Henri Lefebvre argues that all spaces are socially produced and physically experienced, through the sensations of body. Lefebvre suggests that there are different forms of spatial practice, all of which produce, reproduce, codify and symbolise social experience (p. 33). In practice this means that the distinctions between the abstract ideal of an empty, neutral space and the rooted materiality of place are not as sharp as, on first sight, they might appear. This has implications for how the social meanings of place and space might be understood in relation to theatre education. Theatre-makers habitually talk about the 'space' in which they work, by which they usually mean the room used for the workshop or performance (the studio, rehearsal room, classroom, hall). The 'place' is the venue for the work (the school, prison, town hall, youth club or theatre building, for example). In Lefebvre's terms, both articulations of place and space are suffused with association.

Although it has long been understood that the institutions in which theatre education takes place are already deeply resonant with meanings, the social meanings of the space created by theatre-makers within these institutions have received less critical attention. Throughout this book I have referred mainly to schools, but theatre education also takes place in other institutional settings, such as hospitals, prisons, youth clubs and museums, all of which have disciplinary structures. This means that the experience of theatre needs to transgress complex relationships to place within the space in which the practice happens. However, it does not mean that the space of the performance or workshop is 'empty' or necessarily liberating. In his book *Theatre, Education and the Making of Meanings*, Anthony Jackson comments that the combination of the institutional place and the discipline of the performance space can feel oppressive, particularly when audiences are expected to participate in the drama:

> There are perhaps few worse experiences in this field of work than to find oneself belittled or one's dignity undermined within a supposedly participatory event from which there is no ready escape. (p. 8)

This is a wise caution. The idea of the creative theatre educator travelling to liberate children from the oppressive regime of education, if such a myth still exists, not only fails to understand the care that is exercised by those who work in the education system and the stability it can provide but also takes little account of the view that space, as well as place, always intersects with its location and can feel threatening as well as liberating.

This suggests that the idea of place is open to re-interpretation. Place, perhaps most associated with stability, rootedness and belonging, also offers and imaginative way of understanding and perceiving the world. In his book *Place: A Short Introduction* (2004), the cultural geographer Tim Cresswell argues that to understand somewhere as a place is to recognise the complexity of the lives of its inhabitants. This opens the possibility of a social imaginary of a place in which the emptiness of facts and statistics might be replaced by a more nuanced understanding of the connections between people and their environment. Citing Baghdad as an example, Cresswell suggests that to think of it 'as a place is in a different world to thinking of it as a location on which to drop bombs' (p. 11). Conversely, if the meanings applied to particular places become too fixed around particular values or attitudes, what is experienced as a positive sense of belonging for some people can act as a powerful means of exclusion for others. This may take the form of bigotry and racism; on a more personal level, to be told that you should 'know your place' is an act of aggression, designed to belittle and bully. Rather than seeing place as a nostalgic marker of social stability, Cresswell argues that the relationship between place and identity is always in flux. 'Place,' he argues, 'is the raw material for the creative production of identity rather than an *a priori* label of identity. Place provides the conditions of possibility for creative social practice' (p. 39).

The perception that there is a creative dynamic between place and identity is shared by the social theorist Avtar Brah. In her book *Cartographies of Diaspora* (1996), Brah analyses the problematic of 'home', particularly in relation to diasporic or migrant communities. Changing social structures and work patterns have led to complicated family relationships, and increased geographical mobility has led some people to experience a complex sense of belonging to places in different parts of the world. Brah suggests that, as identity is formed in relation to the people we have known and the social networks with which we identify, it is 'always a plural and always in process, even when it might be construed or represented as fixed' (p. 195). This has implications for how a sense of belonging is experienced, particularly by those who have emotional ties to more than one place.

In relation to artistic practice, the idea that contemporary life is characterised by identification with different places and fluid social networks raises political questions about how artists relate to site, place and space. Miwon Kwon's study of site-specific art, *One Place After Another: Site Specific Art and Locational Identity* (2002), is articulated around the central problematic of how to unsettle the nostalgic myth that identities are inevitably fixed and place-bound without replacing it with the equally problematic notion that artists are nomads or tricksters who intervene in different sites but have no expectation of making long-term commitments to the places in which they work. Kwon suggests that it is not a matter of taking sides between place and space, rootedness and nomadism, identity and difference, but recognising that there is a productive and creative tension between them. It is in the gap between these apparent oppositions that there is scope for the imagination to disrupt, trouble or illuminate the dynamic social meanings of place and space. The following example of practice illustrates how this negotiation between self and place can be re-imagined in theatre education.

Interrogating place, representing identity

The site-specific performance *Boychild* investigated place as both a metaphor and a physical location. *Boychild* was performed on Father's Day, 17 June 2007, in the disused Admiralty Underwater Weapons building in Portland, Dorset. The choice of date and place was auspicious; it was the culmination of a year-long project led by performance artist Mark Storor and produced by educationalist Anna Ledgard with more than eighty men and boys from the local area. The project had received some funding from the Wellcome Trust, a charity that supports public engagement with science through the arts, and it was expected to investigate bioethical issues of maleness and masculinity. The performance drew on the expertise of practising scientists to provide information about the workings of the male body. Groups of boys in primary and secondary schools, young men held in a young offenders' institute, fathers-to-be and older men from the local working men's clubs worked creatively in a variety of media to share insights into what masculinity meant to them and to explore their 'place' in the world as men and boys. Invoking the long tradition of learning through theatre, this project integrated scientific learning with more intimate and autobiographical reflections on identity.

Arriving at the disused Admiralty building on the day of the performance, I was immediately stuck by its eerie emptiness. The long, windswept arch of the drive from which I could see the sea, the redundant security barriers and the imposing entrance hall hinted at the orderliness of working lives that had been spent there. The economy of the performance aesthetic and the subtle interrogation of place were established from the beginning. Audiences of ten people were greeted at a side door by the former caretaker of the building. Through the privacy of a headset, we each heard his story, an intimate interweaving of his working years with a more personal retelling of autobiographical events in his life. He watched us listen in silence, isolated from each other by our headsets. A small boy beckoned us into the building, taking us on a journey that would trace life from birth to old age and death. Walking along the corridors, peeping into some rooms and lingering in others was an intense experience. In one room a teenage boy lay in his pyjamas on a beautifully lit mound of unwashed potatoes, carefully turning over one at a time as a recorded poem was played that described the boys' experiences of their bodies in puberty:

> Why do men's hearts give out before women's?
> I dig my hands into the earth, fingers curl
>   around unfamiliar forms.
> As my body sprouts I am an oddly shaped potato.

Connections between scientific questions (why do men's hearts give out before women's?) and the metaphor of the potato illustrating the physical changes of puberty amplified how the learning process had encouraged the boys to make associations between scientific knowledge and their own emotional experiences. Another room similarly captured the complexity of the body through concise use of imagery; the room was unfurnished except for figures and body parts crafted from bread, the imagery of the physicality of life made by fathers and fathers-to-be who had worked with a master baker. The bare rooms and deserted corridors were resonant with images, sounds and activity; the route of the performance drew a symbolic map of the journey of men's lives as they are imagined, experienced and remembered. I found it impossible to move around the building without feeling that I could glimpse the shadows of its former occupants and see the imprints of their working practices, while also remembering the quiet voice of the caretaker who had welcomed us into the building. The social meanings of the space and the aesthetic of the place were in negotiation, and it felt powerful.

Anna Ledgard's account of the process, documented in '*Visiting Time* and *Boychild*: Site-Specific Pedagogical Experiments on the Boundaries of Theatre and Science' (2008), reveals the close alignment between the aesthetic of the workshops and the experience of the promenade performance. Specifically analysing the project in terms of place and space, Ledgard lists the places in which they worked: 'school halls and classrooms, a science centre, a redundant MOD building, a prison education wing, a hospital maternity class, a bakery, a working man's club and even an undertaker's premises' (p. 48). Providing the participants with the opportunity to interrogate how the social meanings of these places had been produced and reproduced was integral to the artistic process and to their learning. Ledgard records how Mark Storor's artistic vision enabled the participants to unfix the familiar meanings associated with the spaces and places in which he worked:

> Storor talks of the importance of transforming space, or 'transgressing it', and a feature of all his workshops is the changing of the space from 'literal' to 'dramatic', from 'expected' to 'unexpected'. (p. 49)

Ledgard describes how this involved rearranging furniture or displaying objects that have a symbolic value, such as vests and pants of different sizes. Ledgard notes Storor's intention to disrupt familiar associations with places, suggesting that 'this "disruption" happens as the perception of space moves from literal to symbolic, having the potential to become the space for new kinds of thinking' (p. 42).

The embodied experience of space, and the use of the physical languages of symbol and metaphor, supported the boys' scientific learning. The personal connections the boys made with biological science and with the experience of maleness was the aspect of the work they commented on most readily in their evaluations. The significance of the experience was articulated publicly by one of the younger participants on the *Guardian* weblog:

> My name is dylan cooper and i am 9 yrs old. I took part in BOYCHILD and i feel one of the luckiest

people in the world to have the chance to do something like this. It has been such a brilliant experience for me, it has really triggered my inner boy and
im sad it has to end. I would like to do BOYCHILD
for the rest of my life. (25 June 2007).

Dylan's suggestion that the project had 'triggered my inner
boy' on first view seems to be a rather trite repetition of language he had heard, but it also suggests that he had been able
to explore his identity in new ways. The adult participants
seemed similarly affected by the experience, although for
them it was a question of unmaking and 'rewriting' their
identities in ways that facilitated new and different connections with each other. This involved, as one adult participant admitted on the weblog, abandoning stereotypical
'male' patterns of behaviour that many of them had performed since childhood. Recalling the mutual support he
had experienced in the project, he wrote:

the BOYCHILD men began rewriting the strands
of our shared emotional DNA ... teasing out the
tightened, twisted and tense strings and gently
curling them between our fingers, stroking them
into shape with breaths deeper than we've drawn
since first walking through the gates of primary
school. (21 June 2007)

The integration of scientific knowledge and the experiences
of daily life enabled the participants to reconsider the journey of men's lives from different perspectives. The process

had moved them beyond the patterns of everyday life into places that, because they felt both familiar and strange, offered them new opportunities for learning and being.

On one level, *Boychild* was a straightforward participatory project that encouraged boys and men to learn about science and bioethical issues through theatre. Its originality lay in how Mark Storor invited the boys and men to use an abstract theatrical language to interweave feelings, scientific questions, biological information, memories, perceptions and imaginings. There were also echoes of the past in this project. The practice was powerfully child-centred, and it was the depth of the experiential learning that meant that the scientific learning became so personally felt. The project built on sustained relationships with people and places; Storor and Ledgard had worked with some of the boys in a previous project in a local hospital. It also deliberately interrogated the social imaginary of place and experience of space. And although this project re-situated the politics of place in the twenty-first century, I could still see the ghosts of the Polish soldiers who had guarded the Bristol docks in 1982.

Theatre education and the creative industries

Theatre education is often complexly poised between different agendas, and particularly between the policies of the government of the day and the social, educational and artistic aspirations of theatre-makers and educators. This remains the case in the twenty-first century, when the rapid pace of technological change and a newly globalised economy are influencing both education and cultural policies. While theatre academics and practitioners have focused on the politics of performative societies, governments across the world have re-branded theatre part of the 'creative industries'. This re-branding represents a significant shift in thinking about the function of the arts, emphasising their economic over their social significance. In her essay 'Nationalising the "Creative Industries"' (2003), Jen Harvie commented on the 'sinister connotations' of the term, observing that it appeared to link theatre to 'the imperialist spread of economic globalization' (p. 16). The creative industries have become instrumental in the regeneration of areas of urban decay, where former industrial areas are branded the 'the new places to be', promoting their cultural assets in the expectation of attracting entrepreneurial investment. The refurbishment of disused factories as arts centres, galleries, museums and theatres is an obvious example of how the cultural sector has been harnessed to an economic agenda.

It is unsurprising, in this climate, that educational policy has been refocused on creativity. Arts educator Ken Robinson, once a major advocate of TIE, has argued that it is the very uncertainty and unpredictability of what the future will look like that should shape twenty-first-century education policies. Speculating on what the world will be like when children who are entering primary school in 2009 reach middle age is an almost futile activity, Robinson argues, and this means that we are educating children for a world that is largely unimaginable. In his book *Out of Our Minds: Learning to Be Creative* (2001), Robinson suggests that young people should be given space to develop their creativity so that they can develop the kind of flexibility of mind that will help them adapt to whatever changing social and economic conditions they face.

The UK Department for Education and Skills report *All Our Futures: Creativity, Culture and Education* (1999), produced by a committee chaired by Robinson, states that the demands of global capitalism require a new kind of workforce and a new form of education. Echoing this impulse, many twenty-first-century education policies are emphasising the need for young people to extend their abilities as creative learners and thinkers. A creative workforce, it is anticipated, will not only contribute to the increasingly profitable 'creative industries' but also be able to respond productively to new business opportunities and apply technological innovations to other areas of work. The UK government explicitly acknowledges that its vision for increased creativity in schools is directly related to the effects of globalisation on the labour market, a view that is perhaps most clearly summarised on its website for teachers, www.teachernet. gov.uk:

> The Government recognises that young people need to develop the creative skills needed in the workplace of the future. Fast-moving technology and global communications call for an ability to produce creative solutions to complex problems. Creative teaching practices can help develop and release pupils' creativity, increasing their ability

to solve problems, think independently and work flexibly. (12 April 2008)

A good example of this policy in practice is the Creative Partnerships scheme, which began in England in 2002 as a direct response to Robinson's report, with initial government funding of £40 million (later rising to more than £150 million). Creative Partnerships aimed to encourage artists and 'creative partners' to work with teachers and young people, particularly in areas of social deprivation. It was designed to revitalise local economies by supporting the cultural sector and, in the medium and long term, to enable young people to become creative-thinking employees. In this conceptualisation, the policy is built on the idea that creative individuals possess marketable skills – variously summarised as the ability to think divergently, to be spontaneous, to be flexible, to take risks and to generate new ideas.

On one level, this renewed interest in creativity in education replicates the 'sinister connotations' that Harvie identifies in her analysis of the creative industries. As Harvie notes, however, theatre-makers have used the government's interest in the creative industries to develop practice that is, in her words, 'impressively socially aware and democratic' (p. 17). Harvie cites the work of regional theatres as an example of practice that has, if not resolved the tension between government economic agendas and cultural activism, found a productive dynamic between the two. The case is similar in theatre education, where new sources of funding for creative learning have enabled theatre practitioners to work with young people in ways that not only are artistically innovative but also encourage new forms of social imagining. Theatre companies such as Third Angel, Blast Theory, Lone Twin and Frantic Assembly are examples of innovative British performance artists who have added to the work of specialist theatre education companies such as C&T and Big Brum. These companies demonstrate a renewed conviction, held passionately in the TIE movement, that innovative theatre practice and education can be connected.

One theatre company that has negotiated the tricky territory between the creative economy and innovative artistic and educational practice is Birmingham-based Stan's Cafe (pronounced 'caff'), a company that specialises in installation and devised performance. Initially inspired by the highly visual and physical aesthetic languages of companies such as Station House Opera, whose work frequently interrogates non-theatrical spaces, Stan's Cafe often integrate 'found' text with film and live performance and develop practice that is responsive to site and place. The company has enjoyed considerable critical success as an experimental theatre company, and its work has toured to venues across Europe and to Hong Kong and Australia. *Guardian* theatre critic Lyn Gardner noted in her weblog entry 'Desperately Seeking Sponsorship' (2007) that the company has become a valued British export; it came second in the Midland World Trade Forum Exporter of the Year Award in 2007, losing out to a company that sells industrial sponges to China.

Arguing that artistic innovation and economic success are not necessarily incompatible, Gardner reminds her readers, 'Art is one of the UK's fastest growing exports – something the government would do well to remember in the upcoming Comprehensive Spending Review.'

Central to the aesthetic principles of Stan's Cafe is an interest in the role of the audience and in finding ways for audiences to make creative connections between the performance and their own experiences. In his essay 'Audiences as Collaborators' (2001) James Yarker, the artistic director of Stan's Cafe, describes the relationship between performers and audiences as a 'partnership', emphasising that the poetics of the company's practice is intended to challenge audiences intellectually and emotionally:

> When I'm in the audience I want my collaborative role to be acknowledged, I hate being taken for granted or being given nothing to do. I don't want to sing or dance-a-long, I don't want to be invited up on stage, I don't want people to come and pick on me, I don't want to be patronised by the notion that pressing a button to make something happen is a meaningful act of collaboration; I want to be given provocative material to work with and space in which to do that work. In respecting, or as Howard Barker would say 'Honouring', the audience as a partner, Stan's Cafe eschews these cheap 'participatory' tricks along with linear narrative and coherent

> messages, instead we invite the creation of per-
> sonal poetic links between passages, motifs and
> ideas. (10 June 2008)

It is interesting, given Howard Barker's criticism of educational theatre, that Yarker mentions his views on the actor—
audience relationship. Yarker's interest in the aesthetics of
audience reception, and in finding meaningful collaborations with audiences, suggests that the company's practice
is particularly well positioned to extend into education. Its
educational work is not separate from other aspects of the
company's artistic output but, as Yarker points out, in 'con-
stant dialogue' with its theatre programme. This means that
the integrity of the company's artistic vision is maintained at
the same time as the performers and devisers are enabled to
extend their practice in new directions with young people.

Stan's Cafe's work in education has been funded by various charitable and public organisations, including Creative
Partnerships, Birmingham City Council and the Wellcome
Trust. One of their education projects, *Plague Nation*
(Birmingham, Nottingham and Bristol, 2004), is a performance installation that developed from their much-toured
gallery piece *Of All the People in All the World* (Warwick
Arts Centre, 2003). In *Plague Nation*, 989 kilograms of rice
were brought into the school hall or gym to symbolise the
population of Britain, one grain for each person. Young
people were invited to weigh out the rice to represent
different statistics, each of which was placed in the space
as an installation. Some statistics were health-related: the

number of people who die each year of measles or AIDS, for example, or whose lives are saved through immunisation programmes. Others charted social statistics researched by the young people, such as the population of their city or school. The carefully labelled piles of rice illustrated the statistics visually, and it was this performative quality that enabled young people to imagine their social meanings: a pile of two million grains of rice on a piece of paper representing the two million children who will die each year from diseases for which there is a vaccine has a powerful emotional impact. As global inequalities were graphically illustrated and played out, the project integrated an understanding of epidemiology with socially aware performance.

Another collaboration with Birmingham primary schools led to *Fruit & Veg City* (Birmingham, 2004), which illustrated how the aesthetic of Stan's Cafe's installations could be used to support children's creative learning. The project involved children making a model city out of fruit and vegetables, a process that entailed closely observing buildings from different angles, visiting a market, designing and making the model city, composing a soundtrack and exhibiting the models in the public space of the market. In their book of instructions about how to turn fruit and vegetables into cityscapes, *Fruit & Veg City* (2006), the children helpfully advise against using tomatoes to make domes as they are 'messy', suggesting instead that 'onions are better and if you need a red dome you can get red onions too' (p. 9). The project encouraged children's development as creative learners and also followed the school's curriculum by exploring the built environment. The installation captured the poetic qualities that characterise the work of Stan's Cafe; there was no linear narrative, no naturalistic characters and no explicit message, but it is evident that the performance of images, textures and cityscapes captured the children's imagination and encouraged them to look at their world from different points of view, both literally and metaphorically.

Education policies that link creative learning to the global economy do not, on the surface, seem to suggest much of a continuum between the radical practices of 1960s TIE and the education work of twenty-first-century theatre-makers. If we look beyond the language of the policies, however, it is clear that developing children's abilities to work creatively does not preclude cultural and social commentary, any more than a theatre in receipt of government subsidy will commission plays that promote party politics. Where there is consonance between the past and the present is in the commitment to experiential learning and to bringing together different areas of the curriculum through artistic practice. The processes and practices may have changed, but this interdisciplinarity, always a feature of TIE, has been recast for the twenty-first century, with artists again working alongside children and teachers to produce innovative education programmes in sustained local partnerships.

Theatre, innovation and education

Earlier in this book I examined Howard Barker's claims that theatre that has an educational purpose lacks a spirit of rebellion, that it is characterised by predictability and predetermined outcomes. Of course, theatre can be rebellious only when it takes risks, and the structures of education sometimes seem to militate against encouraging young people to take risks for themselves. Part of the ambition of this book is to celebrate the inventiveness of theatre-makers whose practice, though often invisible to the wider theatregoing public, frequently has a profound influence on the young people with whom they work. It is also important to acknowledge that theatre-makers have been particularly adept at finding inventive ways to work within the complexity of different institutions and cultural organisations. This means that, in its most adventurous manifestations, theatre that is linked to education is never a compromise between two different value systems, but presents everyone involved with creative opportunities and artistic challenges.

In his study of educational theatre *Theatre, Education and the Making of Meanings*, Anthony Jackson concludes that it will be 'effective educationally only *if* it is effective aesthetically' (p. 160; italics original). This has implications for both theatre form and pedagogy. Early pioneers in TIE developed their practice from progressive education and the activism of counter-cultural theatre, and their successors in theatre education have continued to raise questions about how the processes of working collaboratively and artistically can support young people's learning. Robin Alexander, writing about current teaching practices in his book *Essays on Pedagogy* (2008), advocates a dialogic form of learning, a clear development of active learning that underpins theatre education practices. He describes pedagogy as a 'cultural intervention ... that is deeply saturated with the values and history of the society and community in which it is located' (p. 92). One contribution of theatre education to this form of cultural intervention is to invite critical questioning of these values and histories and to encourage aesthetic engagement with the symbolism of theatre and performance.

The argument of this book is that theatre education practitioners have always undertaken radical experiments in theatre form, and the twenty-first century is no exception. There is a renewed interest in innovative modes of theatrical expression, and this offers young people performance practices that have the potential to disrupt fixed polarities between art and instrumentalism, education and entertainment, popularism and élitism, process and product, activity and passivity, participation and spectatorship. Contemporary theatre education has, at best, a richness and complexity which is multifaceted and textured. Taken together, these innovations in theatre education suggest that young people can be active makers of meaning, creating theatre as they would like life to be rather than simply reproducing the theatre as it already exists.

further reading

Only a few studies are explicitly dedicated to theatre education. The most systematic documentation and critique of the field has been offered by Anthony (Tony) Jackson, who has charted the development of TIE from its beginnings, in *Learning through Theatre: Essays and Casebooks on Theatre in Education* (1980), through to the much revised second edited collection *Learning through Theatre* (1993). His most recent book, *Theatre, Education and the Making of Meanings: Art or Instrument?* (2007), charts educational theatre in a variety of contexts, including museum theatre. Roger Wooster's recent account *Contemporary Theatre in Education* (2007) serves as a helpful introduction to the field, and Kathleen Gallagher and David Booth's book *How Theatre Educates: Convergences and Counterpoints* (2003) offers some insightful accounts by Canadian theatre practitioners and scholars.

The websites of theatre companies that work in education are often illuminating, giving clear accounts of their educational aims and performance methodologies. Good websites are hosted by Stan's Cafe (www.stanscafe.co.uk), Y Touring (www.ytouring.org.uk), Theatre-Rites (www.theatre-rites.co.uk), Oily Cart (www.oilycart.org.uk) and C&T (http://candtnetwork.org). Clips of performances are also available on YouTube, which also invites interaction with its website. Practice is often funded by charities, and evaluations may be published on their websites. Critical analyses of practice have been published in academic journals, particularly in *Research in Drama Education: The Journal of Applied Theatre and Performance*, published by Routledge. The US-based *Journal of Youth Theater* frequently carries articles about theatre education and children's theatre, as does the online Australian journal *Applied Theatre Researcher* (www.griffith.edu.au/arts-languages-criminology/centre-public-culture-ideas/research/applied-theatre/publications/issues).

Theatre education is inevitably interdisciplinary. Books that illuminate the practices of applied and community theatre include Baz Kershaw's *The Politics of Performance: Radical Theatre as Cultural Intervention* (1992), Eugene van Erven's *Community Theatre: Global Perspectives* (2001), Jan Cohen-Cruz's *Local Acts: Community-Based Performance in the United States* (2005) and Helen Nicholson's *Applied Drama: The Gift of Theatre* (2005). For those interested in drama teaching, authors Gavin Bolton, Kathleen Gallagher, Dorothy Heathcote, David Hornbrook, Andy Kempe, Jonothan Neelands, Cecily O'Neill, John O'Toole, Philip Taylor and Joe Winston have written widely on drama in primary and secondary schools. Recent studies of theatre for children include work by David Wood, Stuart Bennett and Shifra Schonmann, whose books are listed below.

Action Pie, Cardiff. *Questions Arising in 1985 from a Mutiny in 1979. Six T.I.E. Programmes.* Ed. Christine Redington. London: Methuen, 1987. 89–114.

Alexander, Robin. *Essays on Pedagogy.* London: Routledge, 2008.

Barker, Howard. *Arguments for a Theatre.* 3rd ed. Manchester: Manchester UP, 1997.

Belgrade Coventry Theatre in Education Company. *Big Deal. Theatre-in-Education: Four Junior Programmes.* Ed. P. Schweitzer. London: Methuen, 1980. 189–232.

————. *The Navigators. A Half-Day Programme for Middle and Top Infants. Theatre-in-Education: Five Infant Programmes.* Ed. P. Schweitzer. London: Methuen, 1980. 55–86.

Bennett, Stuart, ed. *Theatre for Children and Young People.* London: Aurora Metro, 2005.

Boal, Augusto. *Theatre of the Oppressed.* Trans. Charles A. McBride and Maria-Odilia Leal McBride. London: Pluto, 1979.

Bolton, Gavin. *Acting in Classroom Drama.* Stoke-on-Trent, UK: Trentham, 1998.

Bolton Octagon Theatre-in-Education Company. *Sweetie Pie: A Play about Women in Society.* London: Methuen, 1975.

Bond, Edward. 'The Dramatic Child.' *Eleven Vests + Tuesday.* London: Methuen, 1997. 86–93.

————. 'Belgrade TIE'. *Edward Bond Letters.* Ed. Ian Stuart. Los Angeles: Harwood Academic, 1998. 117–212.

————. 'Notes on Theatre-in-Education.' *The Hidden Plot.* London: Methuen, 2000. 56–8.

————. Personal interview with the author. Cambridge, December 2000.

————. *The Hidden Plot.* London: Methuen, 2000.

Brah, Avtar. *Cartographies of Diaspora.* London: Routledge, 1996.

Cohen-Cruz, Jan. *Local Acts: Community-Based Performance in the United States.* New Brunswick, NJ: Rutgers UP, 2005.

Cooper, Dylan. 'At Last – Educational Theatre That Can Be Called
    Art.' Weblog comment. *The Guardian*, 25 June 2008. 22 July
    2008 <www.guardian.co.uk/stage/theatreblog/2007/jun/20/
    sitespecific>.

Cresswell, Tim. *Place: A Short Introduction*. Oxford: Blackwell, 2004.

Dawson, Katie, Sally Vander Ghenyst, Lauren Kane, Nat Miller, Rachael
    Miller, Sarah Rinner, April Gentry-Sutterfield, and Spencer
    Sutterfield. 'Balancing Seasons.' *Theatre for Young Audiences/USA*,
    Fall 2006: 4–12. 12 Nov. 2008 <www.assitej-usa.org/TYA/
    Fall2006/TYA%20Feature%20fall06.pdf>.

Department for Education and Skills (DFES). *All Our Futures: Creativity,
    Culture and Education*. London: Her Majesty's Stationery Office, 1999.

Dewey, John. *Art as Experience*. 1934. New York: Capricorn, 1958.

Edgar, David. 'Where's the Challenge?' *The Guardian*, 22 May 2004.
    21 June 2008 <www.guardian.co.uk/artanddesign/2004/may/22/
    artspolicy>.

Editorial. *Theatre in Education: A Bulletin of the Drama, in University,
    College, School or Youth Group* 1.1 (15 Feb. 1947): 1–7.

Edwards, Ness. 'The Workers' Theatre.' 1930. *Theatres of the Left 1880–
    1935: Workers' Theatre Movements in Britain and America*. Ed. Raphael
    Samuel, Ewan MacColl, and Stuart Cosgrove. London: Routledge &
    Kegan Paul, 1985. 77–98.

Féral, Josette. Introduction. *Substance* 31 (2002): 3–17.

Forestdale Primary School with Stan's Cafe. *Fruit and Veg City*.
    Birmingham: Stan's Café, 2006.

Gallagher, Kathleen, and David Booth, eds. *How Theatre Educates:
    Convergences and Counterpoints*. Toronto: U of Toronto P, 2003.

Gardner, Lyn. 'Desperately Seeking Sponsorship.' *The Guardian*,
    5 Oct. 2007. 12 May 2008 <www.guardian.co.uk/stage/
    theatreblog/2007/oct/05/stagebusinesstheatrecompanies>.

Govan, Emma, Helen Nicholson, and Katie Normington. *Making a
    Performance: Devising Histories and Contemporary Practices*. London:
    Routledge, 2007.

Greig, David. *Dr Korczak's Example*. Edinburgh: Capercaillie, 2001.
    ———. 'Rough Theatre.' *Cool Britainnia: British Political Drama in the
    1990s*. Ed. Rebecca D'Monte and Graham Saunders. Basingstoke,
    UK: Palgrave, 2008. 208–21.

Greig, Noel. *Young People, New Theatre: A Practical Guide to an Intercultural Process.* London: Routledge, 2008.

Harvie, Jen. 'Nationalising the "Creative Industries".' *Contemporary Theatre Review* 13.1 (2003): 15–32.

Heathcote, Dorothy. *Collected Writings on Education and Drama.* Ed. Cecily O'Neill and Liz Johnson. Evanston, IL: Northwestern UP, 1991.

Hornbrook, David. *Education and Dramatic Art.* Oxford: Blackwell, 1989.

Jackson, Tony, ed. *Learning through Theatre: Essays and Casebooks on Theatre in Education.* Manchester: Manchester UP, 1980.

———, ed. *Learning through Theatre.* 2nd ed. London: Routledge, 1993.

———. *Theatre, Education and the Making of Meanings: Art or Instrument?* Manchester: Manchester UP, 2007.

Kempe, Andy, and Marigold Ashwell. *Progression in Secondary Drama.* London: Heinemann, 2000.

Kershaw, Baz. *The Politics of Performance: Radical Theatre as Cultural Intervention.* London: Routledge, 1992.

———. 'Performance and Globalisation.' *Contemporary Theatre Review* 16.1 (2006): 145–7.

———. *Theatre Ecologies: Environment and Performance Events.* Cambridge: Cambridge UP, 2007.

Kwon, Miwon. *One Place After Another: Site Specific Art and Locational Identity.* Cambridge, MA: MIT Press, 2002.

Ledgard, Anna. '*Visiting Time* and *Boychild*: Site-Specific Pedagogical Experiments on the Boundaries of Theatre and Science.' *Creative Encounters.* Ed. Ralph Levinson, Helen Nicholson, and Simon Parry. London: Wellcome Trust, 2008. 36–55.

Lefebvre, Henri. *The Production of Space.* Trans. Donald Nicholson-Smith. Oxford: Blackwell, 1991.

Little, Ruth. *The Young Vic Book: Theatre Work and Play.* London: Methuen, 2004.

Mackey, Sally. 'Performance, Place and Allotments: Feast or Famine?' *Contemporary Theatre Review* 17.2 (2007): 181–91.

Mamet, David. *A Whore's Profession: Notes and Essays.* London: Faber & Faber, 1994.

McCaslin, Nellie. 'History of Children's Theatre in the United States.' *Children's Theatre & Creative Dramatics.* Ed. Geraldine Brain Siks and Hazel Brain Dunnington. Seattle: U of Washington P, 1961. 21–6.

Milne, Geoffrey. 'Theatre in Education: Dead or Alive?' *Our Australian Theatre in the 1990s*. Ed. Veronica Kelly. Amsterdam: Rodopi, 1998. 152–67.

Mueller, Roswitha. 'Learning for a New Society: The *Lehrstück*.' *The Cambridge Companion to Brecht*. Ed. Peter Thomson and Glendyr Sacks. Cambridge: Cambridge UP, 1994. 79–95.

Murphy, Eileen. Introduction. *Sweetie Pie: A Play about Women in Society*. London: Methuen, 1975. 5–23.

Neelands, Jonathan. *Beginning Drama 11–14*. London: David Fulton, 2004.

Nicholson, Helen. 'Acting, Creativity and Justice: An Analysis of Edward Bond's *The Children*.' *Research in Drama Education* 18.1 (2003): 9–23.
———. *Applied Drama: The Gift of Theatre*. Basingstoke, UK: Palgrave, 2005.
———. 'At Last, Educational Theatre That Can Be Called Art.' *The Guardian*. 20 June 2008. 22 July 2008 <www.guardian.co.uk/stage/theatreblog/2007/jun/20/sitespecific>.

O'Connor, Peter, Briar O'Connor, and Marlane Welsh-Morris. 'Making the Everyday Extraordinary: A Theatre in Education Project to Prevent Child Abuse, Neglect and Family Violence.' *Research in Drama Education* 11.2 (2006): 235–45.

O'Toole, John. *Theatre in Education: New Objectives for Theatre – New Techniques in Education*. London: Hodder & Stoughton, 1976.

O'Toole, John, and Penny Bundy. 'Kites and Magpies: TIE in Australia.' *Learning through Theatre: Essays and Casebooks on Theatre in Education*. Ed. Tony Jackson. Manchester: Manchester UP, 1980. 133–50.

Pammenter, David. 'Devising for TIE.' *Learning through Theatre: Essays and Casebooks on Theatre in Education*. Ed. Tony Jackson. Manchester: Manchester UP, 1980. 36–50.

The Plowden Report. *Children and Their Primary Schools*. London: Her Majesty's Stationery Office, 1967.

Ravenhill, Mark. *Citizenship. Shell Connections 2005: New Plays for Young People*. London: Faber & Faber, 2005. 211–69.

Rebellato, Dan. *1956 and All That*. London: Routledge, 1999.

Redington, Christine. *Can Theatre Teach?* Oxford: Pergamon, 1983.
———, ed. *Six T.I.E Programmes*. London: Methuen, 1987.

Report of the Conference on Children and the Theatre. *Theatre in Education: A Bulletin of the Drama, in University, College, School or Youth Group* 1.1 (15 Feb. 1947). 1–3.

Retallack, John. *Company of Angels: Four Plays by John Retallack.* London: Oberon, 2007.

Ricoeur, Paul. *Lectures on Ideology and Utopia.* New York: Columbia UP, 1986.

Robinson, Ken. *Out of Our Minds: Learning to Be Creative.* Oxford: Capstone, 2001.

Schonmann, Shifra. *Theatre as a Medium for Children and Young People.* Dordrecht, Netherlands: Springer, 2006.

Schweitzer, Pam, ed. *Theatre-in-Education: Five Infant Programmes.* London: Methuen, 1980.

———, ed. *Theatre-in-Education: Four Junior Programmes.* London: Methuen, 1980.

———, ed. *Theatre-in-Education: Four Secondary Programmes.* London: Methuen, 1980.

Taylor, Philip. *Researching Drama and Arts Education*: *Paradigms and Possibilities.* London: Falmer, 1996.

———. *Applied Theatre: Creating a Transformative Encounter.* New York: Heinemann, 2003.

Taylor, Philip, and Christine Warner, eds. *Structure and Spontaneity: The Process Drama of Cecily O'Neill.* Stoke-on-Trent, UK: Trentham, 2006.

Teachernet. 'Creativity in Schools.' UK Department for Children, Schools and Families. 28 Feb. 2009 <www.teachernet.gov.uk/management/atoz/C/creativityinschools/>.

Thomas, Tom. 'A Propertyless Theatre for the Propertyless Class.' *Theatres of the Left 1880–1935: Workers' Theatre Movements in Britain and America.* Ed. Raphael Samuel, Ewan MacColl, and Stuart Cosgrove. London: Routledge & Kegan Paul, 1985. 185–204.

Tuan, Yi-Fu. *Space and Place: The Perspective of Experience.* Minneapolis: U of Minnesota P, 1977.

Vallins, Gordon. 'The Beginnings of TIE.' *Learning through Theatre: Essays and Casebooks on Theatre in Education.* Ed. Tony Jackson. Manchester: Manchester UP, 1980. 2–15.

Van Erven, Eugene, ed. *Community Theatre: Global Perspectives.* London: Routledge, 2001.

Whybrow, Nicolas. 'Theatre in Education: What Remains?' *New Theatre Quarterly* 38 (May 1994): 198–9.

——. 'Young People's Theatre and the New Ideology of State Education.' *New Theatre Quarterly* 39 (Aug. 1994): 267–80.

Willett, John, ed. *Brecht on Theatre: The Development of an Aesthetic.* London: Methuen, 1964.

Winston, Joe. *Drama, Narrative and Moral Education.* London: Falmer, 1998.

Witham, Barry B. *The Federal Theatre Project: A Case Study.* Cambridge: Cambridge UP, 2003.

Wood, David. *Theatre for Children.* London: Faber & Faber, 1997.

Wooster, Roger. *Contemporary Theatre in Education.* Bristol: Intellect, 2007.

Yarker, James. 'Audiences as Collaborators.' Transcript of paper given at the New Work Network's conference, 'The Chemistry Experiment', Arnolfini, Bristol, 10 Feb. 2001. 24 Apr. 2008 <www.stanscafe. co.uk/helpfulthings/audiencesascollaborators.html>.

index

acknowledgements

Writing this book has prompted memories of theatre that has inspired generations of young people. Times change, people move on, and I should like to take this opportunity to thank everyone who has shared their insights and creativity with me over many years. In particular, theatre-makers and educators Mark Storor, Anna Ledgard, Claudette Bryanston and Alison New generously shared their practice with me, and I consider myself privileged that Edward Bond kindly agreed to write the foreword to this book. I am indebted to series editor Dan Rebellato and Kate Haines at Palgrave, who have been astute critics and tactful commentators on early drafts of this book. Colleagues and friends James Thompson, Peter O'Connor, Sally Mackey, Simon Parry, Baz Kershaw, Joe Winston, Tony Jackson, Gilli Bush-Bailey and Louise Keyworth have all prompted me to think in different ways. Most especially, I am grateful for the generosity of those whose work continues to sustain me and, to everyone who helped me keep going while writing this book, thank you.

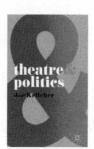

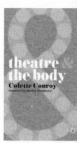